Letts explore

A View from the Bridge

Arthur Miller

Guide written by Ron Simpson

A *Letts* Literature Guide for GCSE

Contents

Contents

Plot summary

1 In the early 1950s Eddie Carbone, a longshoreman, lives in Red Hook, near Brooklyn Bridge in New York, with his wife Beatrice and her niece Catherine.

3 Rodolpho is young, blond, fond of dancing and singing in a high tenor voice. Catherine and he are attracted to each other; Eddie just thinks he is 'weird'.

2 Eddie is too involved emotionally with Catherine. This makes him over-protective of her, but the problems increase when Marco and Rodolpho, Beatrice's cousins from Italy, arrive as illegal immigrants.

9 Marco's honour is outraged. He spits on Eddie and later, in prison, is persuaded with difficulty not to attack Eddie so he can attend the wedding of Rodolpho and Catherine.

10 Marco challenges Eddie; Eddie draws a knife; Marco turns the knife on Eddie, who dies. Catherine and Rodolpho have the chance of a life together in America.

5 Eddie discovers, in an interview with Alfieri, the lawyer, that the law can do nothing about Rodolpho – except as an illegal immigrant.

4 Weeks pass and Rodolpho and Catherine spend their time together, going to the cinema and enjoying themselves. Eddie tells Catherine that all Rodolpho wants from her is American citizenship.

6 Eddie has a symbolic confrontation with the two brothers: trying to humiliate Rodolpho in a boxing bout, then being himself humiliated by Marco in a trial of strength.

8 After another failed interview with Alfieri, Eddie telephones the Immigration Service. Marco and Rodolpho are arrested, together with two relations of another neighbourhood family.

7 At Christmas Eddie, while drunk, discovers Rodolpho with Catherine in her bedroom. In a fury he throws out Rodolpho and Catherine opts to go with him.

Who's who in *A View from the Bridge*

Eddie Carbone

Eddie is the tragic protagonist, meaning that he is the central character whom the tragedy befalls, but is he the tragic hero? Do you find anything heroic in Eddie? The most noble element in his character is that he is always true to himself: 'not purely good, but himself purely', as Alfieri puts it. Eddie has a code of honour (as shown in the story of Vinnie Bolzano), but he breaks this code of honour, destroying his own life and those of others because of his obsession with Catherine. It may be that he genuinely believes Rodolpho to be unsuitable and that he is protecting Catherine from an effeminate opportunist, but before the 'submarines' arrive, his absurdly over-protective attitude to Catherine and his non-existent sex life with Beatrice briefly surface as subjects for argument. Later, Eddie's problems are summed up by Beatrice's questions: (to him) 'When am I gonna be a wife again?' and (to Catherine) 'Was there ever any fella he liked for you?'.

Eddie exists very much as part of a community, and this both gives him his strength and brings about his destruction. He is uneducated and hard-working, determined to do his duty by his family and maintain the respect of his neighbours. He has genuinely been a loving guardian to Catherine and his claims to Alfieri that, when necessary, he went looking for work in Hoboken, Staten Island and so on, ring true. His prejudice against Rodolpho because he is not conventionally manly is shared by his workmates Mike and Louis. Where Eddie ultimately goes wrong is in betraying his code of honour by informing the Immigration Department. He loses all respect and must confront Marco to regain his name: 'Now gimme my name and we go together to the wedding.' Eddie is, in many ways, a normal working man, but, as Alfieri says, he is a victim of 'a passion that had moved into his body like a stranger'.

Beatrice

Beatrice is a simple and good woman whose problems seem almost incidental to the major tragedy of the play. Her problems are <u>domestic</u> and <u>marital</u>, but they are put aside as the Eddie/Catherine/Rodolpho/Marco tragedy works itself out. Her problems, however, are considerable: what has obviously been a fairly successful marriage has deteriorated into emotional and sexual neglect on Eddie's side. Is this in any way Beatrice's own fault? Does she accept too much? It is important that both Catherine ('my sister Nancy's daughter') and the two illegal immigrants are <u>*her*</u> <u>relations, not</u> <u>Eddie's</u>, but she is reduced to pleading and attempting to do good by stealth while their relationships with Eddie plunge headlong into tragedy.

Beatrice becomes involved in events that are too much for her to deal with, in emotions too violent for her to possess, but what of <u>her</u> <u>own</u> <u>standards,</u> <u>opinions</u> <u>and</u> <u>preferences</u>? What are we told of them?

Beatrice seems at first to have <u>potential</u> <u>as</u> <u>a</u> <u>comic</u> <u>character</u>. Her confusions and panics over tablecloths and supper, plus her banter with her husband, are the stuff of many a television sit-com wife. She can at times seem <u>naïve</u>, but Beatrice understands the problem with Eddie and Catherine long before they do, gently chiding the over-protective Eddie or warning Catherine against innocently childish behaviour to Eddie. Her tragedy is that, though everyone likes or even loves her, nobody pays any attention to her. Mostly her role is to suffer, and even her final unusually frank attempts to force Eddie to act sensibly <u>fall</u> <u>on</u> <u>deaf</u> <u>ears</u>.

Catherine

Catherine begins the play in all innocence: she is ready to accept people for what they appear to be, she sees no danger. She is <u>dutiful</u> <u>and</u> <u>loving</u> to her elders, she only thinks of taking a job because the principal advises it (and because she's the school's best pupil)! She happily waves at Louis despite Eddie's warnings. She is eager to break away from home to the extent of taking a job but, even so, her joyful first words after Eddie gives permission are, 'I'm gonna buy all new dishes with my first pay'. The <u>family</u> <u>love</u> between niece and uncle is genuine, but in all innocence Catherine contributes to the unhealthy obsession Eddie is developing: a more worldly girl would understand the effect of walking around in front of him in her underwear. However, the way she dresses in the first two scenes shows her <u>growing</u> <u>maturity</u>: her new skirt ('too short', says Eddie) and her high heels to welcome her cousins (removed on Eddie's orders).

What makes <u>such</u> <u>a</u> <u>sweet,</u> <u>obedient,</u> <u>trusting</u> <u>girl</u> defy Eddie as she does, and drive him to desperation and, indirectly, death? Obviously, Eddie's little girl is growing up and Eddie's own behaviour forces the issue at times, but also Catherine is someone with <u>a</u> <u>capacity</u> <u>for</u> <u>loyalty</u> <u>and</u> <u>devotion</u>. She is devoted to Eddie and Beatrice, but, when Rodolpho appears, the impression he makes on her is increased by her sheltered background: how many young men has she met who have set out to be charming to her? Her devotion to Rodolpho leads to outbursts against Eddie that would have been impossible a few weeks before. Her feelings about Rodolpho are generally clear-cut, but understandably <u>her</u> <u>feelings</u> <u>about</u> <u>Eddie</u> <u>are</u> <u>more</u> <u>complex</u>. In the most erotic scene with Rodolpho, at the beginning of Act 2, her affection for Eddie is still obvious: 'he was always the sweetest guy to me'. To understand the development of Catherine's feelings, you should compare her outburst on pages 80 and 81 ('In the garbage he belongs!') with her last words in the play, as Eddie dies.

Marco

Of all the characters in the play, Marco reveals himself most in his actions, not his words (see if you can find any examples of unnecessary chat from Marco). Marco is strong, frequently silent, devoted to his family, anxious to do right, self-contained, but emotional. His gratitude to his hosts colours his conduct and he gives way on comparatively trivial matters: if Rodolpho's singing is a nuisance or a danger, then Rodolpho should stop singing. His love for his brother is obvious, but he is quite aware of his failings: 'They paid for your courage,' is his reason for Rodolpho's success as a singer, 'But once is enough.' Marco is defined by three moments of physical action when honour is at stake: the chair-lifting, spitting at Eddie and the final challenge to Eddie.

Miller's achievement in the character of Marco is to create a character who commits murder, but is seen as admirable. Marco provokes the confrontation with Eddie, yet he is to be admired. Partly this impression is produced by the reaction of others: his workmates praise him as 'a regular bull', Beatrice tries to restrain Eddie at the end by reminding him, 'You always liked Marco', and Eddie sums him up, 'Marco goes around like a man; nobody kids Marco.' His guilt is also seen to be lessened by the fact that Eddie produced the knife. Above all, though, Marco is prompted not by his selfish interests, but by what he sees as honourable. He follows the same code of honour as Eddie, but he does not deviate from it. In their scenes with Alfieri, the resemblance to Eddie is very striking. Each of them thinks that <u>there</u> <u>should</u> <u>be</u> <u>a</u> <u>law</u> against the sort of behaviour that is troubling them, and in each case Alfieri explains that there is no law against conduct they find offensive. Unlike Eddie, Marco continues to pursue his code – with tragic consequences.

Rodolpho

Like most of the characters in the play, Rodolpho goes on a <u>journey</u> <u>within</u> <u>himself</u>. At the beginning, he is clearly immature and loves telling tall stories, making himself the centre of attention and treating American society like <u>a</u> <u>typical</u> <u>youthful</u> <u>consumer</u>. His first line in the Carbone household is accompanied by the stage direction, 'ready to laugh', though he does at least wait for Marco's nod of approval before launching into *Paper Doll*. As with Catherine, <u>his</u> <u>growing</u> <u>maturity</u> becomes apparent in the first scene of Act 2, not only in their commitment to each other, but in his dignity, his honest assessment of life in America and Italy, and his refusal to indulge in romantic fantasies. The attempted humiliation of Eddie's kiss makes him stronger, and at the end of the play he is the voice of good sense, attempting to act as peacemaker between Eddie and Marco. With his marriage to Catherine, Rodolpho is <u>the</u> <u>success</u> <u>story</u> <u>of</u> <u>the</u> <u>play</u>.

The problem an audience faces with Rodolpho is in deciding whether there is <u>any</u> <u>truth</u> <u>in</u> <u>Eddie's</u> <u>criticisms</u>. Do we accept his answer to Eddie's charge of exploiting Catherine to become a citizen: 'You think I would carry on my back the rest of my life a woman I didn't love just to be an American?'? Eddie also implies that he is homosexual – or, in Eddie's word, 'weird'. The grounds for this are very slight: high tenor voice, blond hair and the ability to mend and cook. But Louis and Mike share Eddie's feelings: 'He comes around, everybody's laughin'.' Do we trust the opinions of Louis and Mike? Perhaps the worst that Rodolpho can be accused of is <u>youth</u> <u>and</u> <u>(to</u> <u>begin</u> <u>with)</u> <u>irresponsibility</u> <u>and</u> <u>extravagance</u>.

Alfieri

Alfieri is <u>less</u> <u>a</u> <u>character</u> <u>than</u> <u>a</u> <u>bridge</u> between the world of Red Hook and that of the audience. Miller tells us very little about him, but the fact that he lived in Italy until the age of 25 is important. He can understand the values of the immigrant community while at the same time he himself belongs in a more sophisticated world. His main purpose is to serve as a <u>chorus</u> figure (see <u>Themes</u> <u>and</u> <u>images</u>) and he provides much more than mere narrative back-up. In particular <u>he</u> <u>establishes</u> <u>the</u> <u>inevitability</u> <u>of</u> <u>the</u> <u>tragedy</u> early on ('sat there as powerless as I and watched it run its bloody course…') and <u>demands</u> <u>attention</u> <u>for</u> <u>the</u> <u>humanity</u> <u>of</u> <u>the</u> <u>characters</u>: 'I think I will love him more than all my sensible clients'.

Apart from his choric function, Alfieri has three scenes, in all of which he reasons with someone who is not prepared to listen to reason. In these scenes he is <u>conventionally</u> <u>liberal,</u> <u>conventionally</u> <u>concerned</u>, but does little more than represent the law which, as he knows, is something alien to these characters: 'In this neighbourhood to meet a lawyer or a priest on the street is unlucky'.

About the author

Arthur Miller

When Arthur Miller's autobiography, *Timebends*, was first published in 1987, much of the press comment was directed at his account of his troubled married life with the doomed film star, Marilyn Monroe. In fact, *Timebends* was speedily recognised as one of the finest accounts of an author's life. As a student of Arthur Miller's plays, you should make sure that your school/college/public library has a copy and at least sample it, with the aid of the index.

Arthur Miller was born in New York in 1915, a first-generation American, his father having emigrated from Poland as a child. Financially affected, like many Americans, by the Great Depression of the 1930s, Miller worked his way through college. Although he began writing plays then, he had to wait for the post-war years for his first successes.

Miller's radical left-wing stance developed from his experiences in the depression years and his awareness of the horrors of fascism in Europe, particularly acute in a Jew only one generation away from Poland. These left-wing views are evident throughout the great quartet of plays that made his reputation. As well as displaying sympathy towards 'ordinary' people, these plays dwell on the need for personal integrity. Above all, they treat the sufferings and deaths of their protagonists as being tragically significant, just like those of princes and heroes. All deal with tragic challenges to conscience endured by imperfect, but not evil, men.

Three of his plays are set in the (then) present. *All My Sons* (1947) searched the conscience of an industrialist who had caused the deaths of American airmen in World War Two by supplying faulty parts. *Death of a Salesman* (1949) explored the broken world of an ageing salesman whose dreams are shattered. Both of the main characters in these plays commit suicide – and, of course, Eddie in *A View from the Bridge* (1955) brings his death on himself. *The Crucible* (1953) was set in 1692, but had a major contemporary theme. Its subject of 17th-century witch trials explicitly relates to the 1950s' purge on Communists and Communist sympathisers.

In 1956 Miller was summoned to appear before the House Un-American Activities Committee. This committee, dominated by Senator Joseph McCarthy, was determined to root out Communists from American life and, just like the Salem witch-trials in *The Crucible*, the way to escape was to give the committee the names of more possible Communists. Miller refused to do this and temporarily lost his passport, but fortunately for him the power of HUAC was soon to wane and he then resumed his career without difficulty.

Arthur Miller can now be seen as the major American playwright of the post-war era. His international reputation is reflected in the constant revivals and new productions of his plays in this country. Throughout the 1990s, work by Miller was frequently staged in London and elsewhere in Britain; *A View from the Bridge* has received many major revivals; the three other early successes are to be seen almost as often; less well-known early plays like *The Man who had all the Luck* prove surprisingly powerful in occasional revivals. *Timebends*, first published in this country by Methuen in 1987, is available in various editions, the most recent a Methuen paperback of 1999.

> *Give me your tired, your poor,*
> *Your huddled masses yearning to breathe free.*

In the late 19th century, these famous words on the Statue of Liberty suggested the welcome that the New World could give to the poor and persecuted of the Old World. The flood of immigrants, whether caused by famine, chronic unemployment, or persecution of Jews (which was happening long before Hitler's death camps), eventually led to a much stricter policy. In 1892, almost in the shadow of the Statue of Liberty, an immigration centre was set up on Ellis Island, to process and accept or reject the hordes of would-be immigrants.

America was widely seen as the land of freedom and opportunity, but very often reality was a great deal more squalid. At the same time, many areas were dominated by one nationality or racial group. So it was with the Italians on the Brooklyn water-front. In particular, the influence of Sicilians brought in strong traditions of family, for both good and ill. 'The syndicate' that arranges the illegal immigrations in *A View from the Bridge* has clear hints of the Mafia and, if its actions in the play seem almost kindly, it must be remembered that the Mafia looks after its own: *Cosa Nostra* (another name for the Mafia) means 'our affair'.

By 1950 the United States was a much more suspicious country than in the previous century. Although the Soviet Union and the United States had been allies in the Second World War, the arms race and the conflict between communism and capitalism brought about the Cold War and spread paranoia about 'Reds' throughout the States. Though Miller escaped the McCarthy-ite 'witch-hunts' comparatively unscathed, many of his colleagues in film and theatre were black-listed, unable to work for years.

This was not a good time to be a left-wing individualist in the United States, but Miller found suppression of the individual in other areas, too – and this is, in part, the background to *A View from the Bridge*. In the Second World War he spent nearly two years working in the Brooklyn Navy Yard and his descriptions of it call up the world of *A View from the Bridge*: a near-majority of Italians in the work force, elaborate treacheries, Sicilian dramas, unpredictable moral codes. Later, he investigated the life of one Pete Panto, a young longshoreman who had attempted to organise a rank-and-file revolt against the alleged Mafiosi of the International Longshoremen's Association. Panto simply 'disappeared' one night. Miller's projected film on the subject came to nothing, but this was another element making up the authenticity of *A View from the Bridge*. Miller himself was shocked at the way the hiring and firing practices of the Brooklyn and Manhattan waterfronts seemed to have been imported from the Sicilian countryside. There, 'a foreman representing the landowners would appear in the town square on his horse' and point to whichever of the humble job-seeking peasants he favoured. In Brooklyn there might have been no town square or horse, but the choice was just as much the result of arbitrary favouritism.

Love

Most of the characters' actions are brought about by love; it is love, not hatred, that fuels the violence. Love is seen in its purest form with Catherine: she is clearly in love with Rodolpho and equally is devoted to Eddie as a 'daughter'. However, even for her, nothing is simple. Not only is her innocent affection for Eddie a partial cause of the tragedy, but it is never absolutely clear what Rodolpho's feelings for her are. Love is also at the heart of Beatrice's problems: her love for Eddie is no longer returned and is increasingly in conflict with her love for Catherine. Love for family is at the heart of Marco's anger against Eddie. But the most obsessive love in the play is Eddie's: as Alfieri says, 'there is too much love for the daughter, there is too much love for the niece'.

Family

Family loyalties are a major factor in the play, but the concept of 'family' can be sinister as well as comforting. Of course there is the horrific tale of Vinny Bolzano ('And they spit on him in the street, his own father and his brothers'), but the family (complete with godfather) is equally the unit of Mafia organisation. At the beginning, Alfieri mentions Sicilians and gangsters in the same speech; the audience is prompted to make this connection. Among the assumptions of the Mafia is the idea that the law is useless and that direct 'justice' is more effective. In business as well as in criminal activity, 'family' members are protected; enemies and those who betray the family are treated ruthlessly. The tragedy in *A View from the Bridge* is not caused by the Mafia, but these concepts exist side by side with more orthodox family ties.

Honour

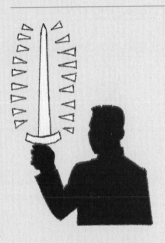

Honour must be maintained; that is the inevitable consequence of the attitudes to family in this play. Insults to the family must be avenged; that is the basis of the vendetta or blood feud. Apart from family honour, Miller also deals with personal honour: name and identity. John Proctor, in *The Crucible* (written two years before *A View from the Bridge*), refuses to sign his name to a dishonest document that could save his life, using the words, 'How may I live without my name?'. Miller's own response before the House Un-American Activities Committee was very similar. The last three pages of *A View from the Bridge* are full of names and lines like, 'I want my name'.

Justice and the law

Justice and the law are not the same thing, and the conflict between them runs through the play. The problem is increased by the fact that the first generation Americans of Red Hook do not really believe in the law, anyway. Alfieri fails totally to convince Eddie and Marco that 'there is no other law' outside the statute book. They cannot relate 'his' law to their code of honour and concept of justice. The irony is that breaking the law is often done for the best of motives, whereas Eddie uses the law in a vindictive mood of jealousy. Perhaps American law can work; perhaps Red Hook justice can work; the combination of the two, though, can bring only tragedy.

The chorus

Arthur Miller originally saw this play as being modelled on a Greek tragedy. The most striking feature of that is his use of a chorus. In Greek tragedy a group of anonymous citizens informed the audience of events before the play, narrated off-stage happenings, commented on the characters, established norms of behaviour, told the audience what to think and even what was going to happen. This is the role filled by Alfieri in *A View from the Bridge*. He is a sort of super-chorus: he does everything a chorus would, but in addition he has a name and personality and takes part in the action at times. Alfieri is particularly effective as a bridge between audience and action: he is himself an Italian immigrant, but as a representative of the despised law he belongs in the audience's world. The play's title is very interesting: it is about the world as seen from the shadow of Brooklyn Bridge, but also as seen from the bridge between old Europe and the New World – and Alfieri's commentary comes from that bridge.

Male and female roles

The world of *A View from the Bridge* is very much an old-fashioned male-dominated society. The men do hard physical labour, and the women look after the men. Though Catherine takes a job, Eddie's comment to Beatrice sums up the older generation's attitudes: 'You lived in a house all your life, what do you know about it? You never worked in your life.' Eddie sees it as his duty to support the family and expects to be obeyed. The difficulties within the marriage finally explode when a woman, Catherine, reveals a mind of her own. Just as women are expected to fulfil an established role, concepts of masculinity are equally traditional, as in the macho confrontations between Eddie and Marco or the way in which Rodolpho is seen as an outsider.

Text commentary

Act One

Arthur Miller originally wrote the play in one act, wishing the action to be continuous. Eventually, on grounds of length, he divided it into two acts, but it is still one continuous story, expressing a single tragic process. There are, however, considerable gaps in time, covered by Alfieri's links. To assist you, this commentary presents the texts in segments which emphasise the 'real' time scale. As there are no separate scenes, the sections are indicated by page references taken from the Penguin (1961, reprinted in Penguin Classics 2002) edition of A View from the Bridge/All My Sons.

Pages 11–13

> **The front is skeletal entirely.**

The set remains unchanged throughout the play. It is what is known as a **composite set**; that is to say, it includes different elements within one unit. From this we learn that the action will take place in different areas. There is one dominant setting: Eddie's apartment. Eddie's living-room is the only naturalistic piece of staging, complete with doors, furniture and so on. This places Eddie's family at the centre of the drama.

However, the family is not the entire drama. The life of the community is also significant and the apartment is seen through the 'skeletal' front of a tenement: the stairway and the telephone booth will become important in Act Two, Alfieri's office will be the scene for two crucial scenes with Eddie, and the prison and outdoor scenes take place in anonymous stage space. The set surrounding the apartment need not be realistic (note Miller's use of the word '**represents**'). Two

London productions in the 1990s opted, respectively, for a complicated and menacing apartment block and a bare setting with the living room raised up like a stage (or a boxing ring).

> **66** *You see how uneasily they nod to me?* **99**

 Alfieri has a <u>**choric**</u> function, performing the role of the Chorus in a Greek tragedy. To do this effectively he has to know a great deal about the characters and action, but he communicates with the audience (if anything) more effectively than with the other characters. Much of his speaking takes the form of <u>**soliloquies**</u>, in other words, <u>**'talking alone' to the audience**</u>. In this scene, Louis and Mike are also on stage, but Alfieri is effectively alone during his speech.

> **66** *But this is Red Hook, not Sicily.* **99**

The characters are poised between being Italian and being American. Eddie's father came from Italy (doubtless his name is really 'Eduardo Carbone') and Beatrice has relatives in the homeland. Rodolpho sets about 'becoming an American' and Alfieri is an Italian who has been in the USA for maybe 30 years. Here he emphasises the Italian tradition.

Explore

Al 'Scarface' Capone (1899–1947) was born in Naples, Italy, spent his youth in New York City and transferred his criminal activities to Chicago in 1920. His career, somewhat fictionalised, has often appeared on screen, notably in *Scarface*.

Alfieri tells the audience that his practice is 'entirely unromantic', that his clients are prepared to 'settle for half', but the words <u>**'and yet…'**</u> in the final paragraph on page 12 prepare us for something different. In a deliberately awkward and twisted sentence he invokes the past to tell us that the tragedy is inevitable – and then he introduces Eddie.

Pages 13–25

The impact of this scene comes from the contrast between a family behaving normally and the air of menace that hangs over what should be normal tea-time activities. The scene is set for the inevitable tragedy. First we have Alfieri's warnings, then the danger that lies in the illegal immigrants, finally the strangeness in Eddie and Catherine's relationship.

And yet much of the <u>dialogue</u> and <u>humour</u> could be considered normal family behaviour. Analyse for yourself the signs of Catherine's affection, her desire to please and to help, the indications that Beatrice and Eddie have developed their relationship over a long time and the humour and teasing between people who know (and like) each other.

> *Katie, I promised your mother on her deathbed. I'm responsible for you.*

Already, at our first sight of them together, it is clear that Eddie's feelings for Catherine have tragic potential. We ought to consider from the start just what these emotions are.

A View from the Bridge went through many versions before completion and, at first, Arthur Miller's main concern was (in his own words) with <u>'the mysterious world of incestuous feelings and their denial.'</u>

Alfieri, our 'chorus', sums up Eddie very well near the end of Act One: 'We all love somebody, the wife, the kids – every man's got somebody that he loves, heh? But sometimes ... there's too much. You know? There's too much, and it goes where it mustn't.' The stage direction when Eddie finally agrees to Catherine taking the job presents his feelings more sympathetically: '<u>with a sense of her childhood,</u> her babyhood, and the years.'

Explore

'For years I unthinkingly thought of Catherine as his daughter. In fact she isn't, so there is no incestuous feeling, but in my mind there was.' (Arthur Miller)

It is impossible to deny Eddie's sexual desire for Catherine and, though he is <u>not a blood relation</u>, it still seems incestuous because he has taken on the role of father. He has even been a good 'father' to her. It is not difficult to find examples in this section of her trust and confidence in him and of his kindness towards her.

Maybe Eddie has reason to worry about Catherine taking a job on Nostrand Avenue, maybe not, but the main indication of his **over-heated** **concern** for her comes early in the scene when admiration for her new hairstyle turns into disapproval of her new dress and her way of walking down the street.

Note that, as well as repeating accusations of 'walking wavy' and drawing men's attention, Eddie describes his own feelings: she gives him **'the willies'** and **'aggravates'** him. He is being protective, certainly, but this is also something that disturbs him emotionally. The situation is complicated because, while he wants her to stay *his* little girl, part of her feels the same way. When Catherine is 'almost in tears', it is not because he has bullied her, but **because he** **disapproves** – Eddie's good opinion is so important to her.

Explore

In this section of the play, which of the two (Eddie and Catherine) more frequently touches the other affectionately? You may be surprised.

Eddie's feelings are complex and contradictory. His relationship with Catherine is doomed. She is, to him, special and should be able to look forward to something more exciting than the traditional female role of tending to the needs of the male provider. Already Eddie sees her working **'someplace in New York in one of them nice buildings'**. His love, both paternal and sexual, drives him to desire different scenarios for her – unless he is simply making excuses to put off the day when she takes a step into the adult world.

> **And they spit on him in the street, his own father and his brothers.**

When Eddie breaks the news of the arrival of Beatrice's cousins, all is happiness: Catherine claps her hands, Beatrice's state is described as **'unutterable joy'**. But very soon comes the warning: 'if everyone keeps his mouth shut,' all will be well: 'nothin' can happen'.

Later Eddie builds up the tension as the merest hint drives him to worry about the women not understanding the power of the United States Immigration Bureau. Finally, Eddie launches into the <u>Vinny Bolzano</u> story.

This is, of course, <u>a foretaste of Eddie's own story</u>. As such, brief as it is (less than a page of text), it is of major importance. It is Eddie who speaks the line that later applies to his own dishonour and the loss of his own good name: 'How's he gonna show his face?' Ironically, Eddie finds it horrifying now. Consider what it is that makes Vinny Bolzano's story so horrifying. After all, nobody dies, unlike the story we are watching, but there is no doubt of the impact of Vinny's tale. Why?

> ❝*Because most people ain't people. She goin' to work; plumbers; they'll chew her to pieces if she don't watch out.* ❞

Look closely at the way Eddie speaks, <u>his rhythms, vocabulary and syntax</u>. Eddie's speech tends to be staccato, ungrammatical (like most of the characters), full of energy, suppressed tension, emotion and the hint of violence. One of Arthur Miller's great skills lies in <u>finding poetry or drama in the speech of ordinary people</u> (re-read Eddie and Beatrice telling Vinny's story), but he is also adept at matching speech patterns to character. Compare the speech patterns of Alfieri, Eddie and Catherine and see how you can distinguish them.

> ❝*You're the one is mad.* ❞

By the end of this scene, the harmony has gone: even Beatrice (who has been unusually forceful in telling Eddie to let Catherine grow up) is out of sympathy with Eddie. Catherine is almost guilty and doing jobs with embarrassed eagerness. Beatrice turns away from Eddie, her chores provide an escape. As for Eddie, he sits staring at cigar smoke and checking his watch: there's more than one way in which <u>time</u> <u>is</u> <u>passing</u> <u>quickly</u>.

Pages 26–33

Look at the introduction to this section. Alfieri tells us that time has passed. He also, in three sentences, gives an <u>ominous</u> <u>edge</u> to this meeting. His speech, both vocabulary and sentence construction, is almost Biblical in its simplicity (note the use of 'And' to start a sentence). Is there something Biblical about the story that is unfolding?

> **❝She said they were poor!❞**

What is poverty? In the previous section Eddie, in a fine statement of the very principles of honour that he will betray, said, '…suppose my father didn't come to this country, and I was starvin' like them over there…and I had people in America could keep me a couple of months? The man would be honoured to lend me a place to sleep.'

The people of Red Hook are <u>poor</u>; the people of Marco's village are <u>starving</u>. However, unlike Rodolpho (who immediately decides that he has rich relatives), Marco can see the truth. Marco understands that 'it's not so good here either' and, in a rare display of emotion, is near to tears when thanking Eddie. He knows that sacrifices have to be made. Can you find other examples of Marco trying to spare the Carbones' expense and inconvenience?

Explore

Probably the best film dealing with the docklands Mafia is *On the Waterfront*, set in New Jersey. It is almost exactly contemporary with *A View from the Bridge* and directed by a famous Arthur Miller collaborator, Elia Kazan.

The presence of the wider 'family' is obvious here, though not particularly threatening. Tony is helpful, but clearly in charge. The <u>importance</u> <u>of</u> <u>'paying</u> <u>them</u> <u>off'</u> will keep Marco and Rodolpho in work. As yet there are no problems, but their arrival owes as much to an illegal organisation as to relatives' generosity.

> **❝How come he's so dark and you're so light, Rodolpho?❞**

The contrast between the brothers is immediate and striking, not only physically, but in their personalities. Marco will show himself powerful by his actions. His words are <u>unfailingly modest</u> – and <u>few</u> in number. He is moved by gratitude and the thought of sending money to his wife, but otherwise the little he says deals mostly with practical matters and his desire not to be too much trouble – and to avoid Rodolpho being too much trouble! He is affectionate towards his brother and takes the elder brother role conscientiously (giving permission to sing), but can you find signs that he is familiar with, and possibly amused by, Rodolpho's exaggerations?

The contrast with Marco makes Rodolpho seem even more unusual. At first the only sign of difference in Rodolpho is his <u>blond hair</u>. Italians are supposed to be dark, but he claims that the Danes invaded Sicily. It is not until later that Eddie drops hints that it may be dyed. Rodolpho is <u>young, immature and excited</u>: is it surprising that he enjoys being the centre of attention? Perhaps his behaviour is rather trivial in the circumstances, but Catherine finds it charming.

Explore

Do you think there is any truth in Eddie's hints? Why does Eddie claim Rodolpho's hair may be dyed?

Rodolpho is a <u>performer</u>: he laughs a lot; he tells a story with imagination and a sense of audience – note the <u>similes</u> (comparisons) in 'listening to the fountain *like birds*'/'The horses in our town are *skinnier than goats*'; he loves to exaggerate, as in the tales of the motorcycle and singing at the hotel; he sings *Paper Doll* (he is already half converted to American culture!) in a very high tenor voice. Like much popular music, this is a <u>love song</u>.

How close to the truth are Rodolpho's stories and boasts? The account of the taxis is probably truthful, enhanced by a vivid and dramatic style of expression. The dream of buying a motorcycle is essentially <u>fantasy</u>. Marco's comments make it clear that the story of singing at the hotel is basically accurate, but less of a triumph than Rodolpho claims.

Because we never had no singers here ...

On page 29 a stage direction, as so often in Miller's plays, is of great help to actor, producer and student alike: _'he is coming more and more to address Marco only'_. From that point, examine the number and type of contributions that Eddie makes and you will find strong indications that he does not consider Rodolpho worth talking to. Now examine what he says following his interruption of _Paper Doll_ and decide why he reacts the way he does and whether what he says and how he behaves are reasonable. You might, for instance, consider that the interruption is perfectly justified ('you don't want to be picked up, do ya?') and Marco supports Eddie in this. But, once again, examine the stage directions which are an excellent guide to Eddie's feelings and motives – as is his attitude to Catherine.

Explore

Eddie calls Catherine 'Garbo'. Greta Garbo was a beautiful and mysterious film star of the 1930s.

You like sugar?'
'Sugar? Yes! I like sugar very much!

Is Catherine's response to Rodolpho any more balanced? She reacts to his blond hair as a miracle ('wondrously', says the stage direction), she finds his singing 'terrific' (she is 'enthralled', we are told) and she very quickly checks that he is not married. Is there anything in Catherine's background that makes her so ready to fall in love at first sight?

What is beyond doubt is that the tragedy is underway. Eddie's attempts to come between Rodolpho and Catherine are doomed. As the section ends, Rodolpho flatters her with a flirtatious confidence carried over from _Paper Doll_; she offers sugar and he accepts readily. The symbolism is none the worse for being obvious (they are 'sweet on one another') and Eddie's face is puffed with trouble.

Quick quiz 1

Who? What? Why? When? Where? How?

1   Who informed on his own uncle?

2   What did Rodolpho do in place of Andreola?

3   Why does Tony warn Marco and Rodolpho to be careful?

4   When does Marco hope to return to Italy?

5   Where is the firm that Catherine hopes to work for?

6   How does Eddie know that the immigrants will get plenty of work?

Who said ... about whom?

1   'He sang too loud.'

2   'Very nice man.'

3   '(he) was learning his trade on these pavements.'

4   'They got stool pigeons all over this neighbourhood.'

5   'You're the Madonna type.'

6   'He trusts his wife.'

Open quotes

Find and complete the following:

1   'And now we are quite civilised...'

2   'The horses in our town are...'

3   '...she's seventeen years old...'

4   'My wife – she feeds them...'

What is...

1   the subway (page 19)?

2   a Buick (page 22)?

3   the syndicate (page 24)?

> ❝*Eddie Carbone had never expected to have a destiny.* ❞

Before the lovers return from the cinema, an extended <u>choric</u> section lets the audience see how deep-rooted are the troubles that have come to the Carbones in two weeks.

During Alfieri's five-line speech, Eddie changes in many ways: time has passed, his stage position is different, but above all he has <u>gained a destiny</u>. A course of action is mapped out for him that he must follow. Note how cleverly Miller tells us that an ordinary man can be a <u>tragic protagonist</u>: it is not essential to be a king, a general or a great lover. Eddie expected to spend his life working, eating, going bowling; now he has to work out his destiny.

> ❝*That's a nice kid? He gives me the heeby-jeebies.* ❞

The situation regarding Rodolpho has developed in the two weeks since he arrived. Arthur Miller now uses the <u>composite set</u> to move easily from the house doorway to the street to inside the house. With one important exception, all the conversation is about Rodolpho and, in the way it tells the audience what has happened and offers alternative views on events, it <u>complements Alfieri's choric function</u>.

In conversation with Beatrice, Eddie's main worry is not that Rodolpho is looking for a passport, though he does mention the problem of his 'advertising himself' (so risking capture) and worries that 'he's taking her for a ride'. What really troubles Eddie is that <u>Rodolpho is 'weird'</u>. Examine the build-up from his worrying about their late return (at 8 o'clock!) through sentences like 'He gives me the heeby-jeebies' and obsessive ravings about Rodolpho's blond hair and his singing, to the conclusive statement (near the bottom of page 35), 'For that character I didn't bring her up.'

Explore

The characters who are little more than walk-ons (like Louis and Mike) outnumber the 'real' characters. They aid the chorus effect by showing us what the community is thinking. Compare Eddie's view of Rodolpho with those of Louis and Mike. Is Eddie affected by their views?

Eddie's <u>views</u> on Rodolpho do not change between his conversation with Beatrice and the one he has outside with Louis and Mike, but his <u>role</u> <u>in</u> <u>the</u> <u>conversation</u> does. He is no longer the one leading the criticism; now he is embarrassed to receive it.

Rodolpho is described as 'funny'. What does 'funny' mean here: '<u>funny</u> <u>peculiar</u>' <u>or</u> '<u>funny</u> <u>ha-ha</u>' or both? Note the word-games that Miller plays with 'funny', 'sense of humour' and so on. The comments of Louis and Mike remain vague because of the frequency of phrases like, 'Well, he ain't exackly funny' and, 'I don't know … he was just humorous'. Is Rodolpho outside their previous experience? Do they lack the words to describe him?

Marco at this stage is not only no trouble for Eddie, he is respected by all because he is a '<u>regular</u> <u>bull</u>'. Marco fits in with the concept of how a man should behave; no one laughs at him.

> ❝No, everything ain't great with me … I got other worries.❞

The attention moves away from Rodolpho only briefly, when Beatrice responds to Eddie's increasing demands that she should worry about Catherine's love affair. She cites her own worries: that <u>sexual</u> <u>relations</u> with Eddie have broken down. Eddie retorts with <u>feeble</u> <u>excuses</u> (he's not well, the 'submarines' bother him), but these have no foundation. Beatrice points out that the situation has applied for three months, not the two weeks since Marco and Rodolpho arrived. In the end Eddie (the man and traditionally in charge) simply refuses to discuss the matter. It is more than interesting that Beatrice's very next words remind us that Catherine is <u>nearly</u> <u>18</u>.

Clearly it is important that this discussion of Eddie's sexual inactivity is placed in the middle of a conversation in which he is arguing against Catherine's romance.

Why does Eddie object to Catherine's romance:
- because Rodolpho is weird;
- because he thinks Rodolpho is after a passport;
- because his desire for Catherine is such that he is unable to be a husband to Beatrice;
- or, even as Beatrice suggests, because he cannot accept Catherine growing up ('What're you gonna stand over her till she's forty?)?

> **❝ I would like to go to Broadway once, Eddie ❞**

Explore

Catherine says they didn't go to 'New York'. Isn't Brooklyn New York? Yes, officially, but Brooklyn used to claim to be the USA's fourth biggest city (over 2 million inhabitants) and Manhattan seems like a different city.

The lovers return happily, Catherine excited (by the film, she says), Rodolpho eager to see Broadway (but very polite in asking). Both are amused by the differences between Italy and Brooklyn (no fountains, no orange trees). Eddie questions Catherine, but avoids confrontation with her. However, he wants <u>no conversation</u> <u>with</u> <u>Rodolpho</u>. Though Rodolpho attempts pleasant talk, all that Eddie is prepared to say to him is to warn him off going to Times Square and to <u>ask</u> <u>him</u> <u>to</u> <u>leave</u> so that he can talk to Catherine.

Fairly soon Rodolpho takes the hint and goes for a walk, becoming <u>a</u> <u>topic</u> <u>for</u> <u>conversation,</u> <u>not</u> <u>a</u> <u>character</u> <u>on</u> <u>stage</u>. Once again we see him through others' eyes. Which is the real Rodolpho?

Eddie's refusal to talk to Rodolpho means that, as for much of this section, two people are left alone on stage.

<u>Dialogue</u> is speech involving more than one person. <u>Duologue</u> has a

similar meaning, except that the conversation is specifically <u>between</u> <u>two</u> <u>people</u>. This section is made up almost entirely of duologues, beginning with Eddie and Beatrice, though there is the short Eddie/Louis/Mike dialogue. Note how the duologue format is maintained when the lovers enter. Louis and Mike leave as Catherine and Rodolpho enter. There are now three on stage, but Rodolpho soon leaves.

Eddie's duologue with Catherine builds to a climax; she rushes into the house. After two short explosive lines, Eddie leaves the house. Once again, a duologue ensues, this time between Beatrice and Catherine.

Catherine need not <u>yet</u> choose between Eddie and Rodolpho, but already she must make important decisions. Is she to continue to believe the man whom she has trusted all her life? Can she prepare herself to say goodbye to Eddie? The girl who shouts 'I don't believe it' at Eddie finds herself, at the end of this section, 'at the edge of tears, as though <u>a familiar</u> <u>world</u> <u>had</u> <u>shattered</u>'.

> **❝I don't see you no more. I come home you're runnin' around someplace – ❞**

Eddie wants to resume the relationship he has had with Catherine: what was, <u>at least on the surface</u>, a friendly family relationship. Hence the attempts at smiles – and, on Catherine's side, the friendly arm-punch. We all know the situation where we try to keep a conversation on a safe subject, but our real feelings (of envy, jealousy or worry, perhaps) force us into <u>using the wrong words</u>. Eddie is obsessed by his love and his destiny. Do you think it is much more difficult for him to keep to the conversation he wants to? Look at the way he presents Catherine's failings: 'I bless you and you don't talk to me', 'I don't see you no more' and other similar statements. What does this suggest about Eddie's feelings and how he feels Catherine has let him down?

Over-riding Catherine's protests and excuses, Eddie lets his obsession burst out in ever more violent form. It starts with him saying that Rodolpho should ask permission, goes on to the passport accusation, to descriptions of Rodolpho as a hit-and-run guy involved in a racket (Mafia hints?), to the final, simple declaration: 'the guy is **no good**!' You should think how much evidence there is for what Eddie says about Rodolpho. You should also examine the speech on page 41 beginning 'You don't think so!' as the words of **a man out of control**.

> ❝*It's wonderful for a whole family to love each other, but you're a grown woman and you're in the same house with a grown man.*❞

The **key words** in the duologue between Beatrice and Catherine are 'baby', 'little girl' and 'grown woman'. Catherine is not guilty in any real sense of the word, but Beatrice makes it clear that she has helped to foster Eddie's feelings for her, not deliberately, but by her **girlish affection**.

When Catherine walks around in front of Eddie in her slip or talks to him when he is in the bathroom in his underwear, it is the act of **an innocent who sees him as a 'father'**, but it helps to inspire **guilty feelings** in Eddie. You will have noticed how reluctant Catherine is to do anything to hurt Eddie: the 'happy families' situation that means so much to him has been real. Despite the upset he has caused over Rodolpho, she still says, 'It just seems wrong if he's against it so much.'

What Beatrice says now is **unfailingly right**. The message is that Catherine is a grown woman and must act like one. She does not wish to fight Eddie, but her future is with Rodolpho. Where Beatrice is at fault is in leaving this excellent advice till **too late**: she has tried, but failed, twice before. What can Beatrice do now? What could Beatrice have done in the months before Marco and Rodolpho arrived? This poor timing is **her contribution to the tragedy**.

Explore

Compare Eddie's reaction to 'you're just jealous' (page 34) with what Beatrice says on page 44: 'he thinks ... maybe I'm jealous', etc.

35

Pages 45–50

> **It was at this time that he first came to me.**

It is in this scene that the certainty of coming horror grips the audience. Pause before considering it to remind yourself of the problem. There is a crime here, but it is not the crime that is destroying the characters. After all, Eddie and Rodolpho are on the same side (<u>so far</u>) in the matter of illegal immigration.

Although Alfieri takes part in this section as a normal character, he does not abandon his chorus role. He introduces Eddie with a brief speech and links up to the next section with another of his soliloquies. His <u>certainty</u> <u>of</u> <u>disaster</u> communicates itself to the audience. Notice, in his first speech, the way in which Eddie's destiny has already taken him over: it is <u>as</u> <u>though</u> <u>he</u> <u>had</u> <u>already</u> <u>committed</u> <u>the</u> <u>crime</u>, he is filled with <u>guilt</u> <u>and</u> <u>revenge</u>. A striking simile here is 'His eyes were <u>like</u> <u>tunnels</u>'. It is the sort of phrase that offers many different meanings, all menacing.

Explore

What do you think 'like tunnels' means? Compare your view with those of your friends and classmates.

The speech that leads to the next stage of the action (pages 49–50) is worth careful study, as <u>the</u> <u>perfect</u> <u>definition</u> <u>of</u> <u>the</u> <u>inevitability</u> <u>of</u> <u>tragedy</u>. Tragedy on stage (notably, though by no means only, <u>Greek</u> tragedy) depends on the audience's knowledge that these things will certainly happen and that witnessing them becomes a <u>purging</u> <u>of</u> <u>the</u> <u>emotions</u>, almost a ceremony. The wise old woman here reminds us that the Gods looked down on Greek tragedy. Now ask yourself: why is this tragedy inevitable?

> **I don't quite understand what I can do for you. Is there a question of law somewhere?**

If you examine what Alfieri says to Eddie throughout the scene, you will find these ideas repeated again and again. Alfieri's key words are 'law', 'legal(ly)', 'proof/provable' and 'nothing' (as in <u>nothing to be done</u>).

Eddie, on the other hand, uses such phrases as 'I know', 'I see', 'I mean' and 'Right?' (in the sense of confirming agreement). They are talking about <u>two</u> <u>different</u> <u>types</u> <u>of</u> <u>evidence</u> and there is no way that the law can solve Eddie's problem. Alfieri is not unsympathetic and gives Eddie some good advice (the same as Beatrice gave him), but his message that there is no law for what Eddie is thinking about shocks Eddie and forces him to seek his own solution.

> ❝ *The guy ain't right, Mr Alfieri.* ❞

There are several reasons why Eddie so often changes his objections to the Rodolpho/Catherine relationship. In part, though, his apparent indecision stems from the fact that he is not articulate enough to put over the ideas he feels, so he simply describes Rodolpho as 'weird'. Here he goes further than he has done so far in specifying <u>Rodolpho's effeminacy</u>.

Explore

What would Eddie think of a man who talks of kissing another man who is sweet and angelic – and eventually does so?

Now Eddie struggles, in speeches that grow longer as his furious obsession drags out every last detail that is troubling him, to explain that Rodolpho 'ain't right'. Starting with his blond hair and slight build, he moves on to his high tenor voice, dressmaking skills and angelic appearance. Do you find any of these convincing? Would you agree that many of these concerns reveal more of Eddie than of Rodolpho? What sort of a man condemns dressmaking as unfit for men?

Eddie Carbone is very mixed up, but it is still clear to him that he <u>must</u> <u>not</u> <u>lose</u> <u>face</u> in front of his fellow-workers: 'Paper Doll/Blondie' is a liability.

> **There's too much, and it goes where it mustn't.**

Alfieri does not wish to be unhelpful, but the law cannot do anything. While insisting that he cannot help, he gives <u>two pieces of advice</u>. As a lawyer, he feels compelled to mention the one course of action with which the law can offer some help to Eddie. 'There's only one legal question here,' he says, and he and Eddie know that neither wants to do anything about the <u>illegal entry</u>. However, the idea is planted in Eddie's mind.

The second piece of advice is good, if only Eddie could accept it. There are <u>three crucial speeches</u> from Alfieri on pages 48 and 49. The speech beginning 'Eddie, I want you to listen to me…' presents the <u>clearest summary of Eddie's condition</u> from a sympathetic point of view. The next speech ('The child has to grow up and go away…') echoes Beatrice's earlier words to Catherine: 'You're a woman, that's all…and now the time came when you said good-bye.' On the next page, he puts it less charitably: 'She can't marry you, can she?' Eddie, predictably, is <u>furious</u> at this.

> **I'm a patsy, what can a patsy do? I worked like a dog twenty years so a punk could have her…**

Do we feel sympathy for Eddie? 'Sympathy' can mean either <u>pity/sorrow</u> or <u>fellow feeling/agreement</u>. Perhaps we have no sympathy with his views on Rodolpho or his attempts to bring the law to bear on him. It is difficult, though, not to have sympathy for the helpless man who is convinced that his little girl has been stolen from him. Re-read Eddie's long speech beginning 'What can I do?' on page 49 and decide if he has a case.

> **It's wonderful. He sings, he cooks, he could make dresses...**

By using <u>symbols</u> authors can make one thing represent another, often more important or powerful thing. Objects can symbolise ideas and people can be symbolised by details. Here, in this last section of Act One, <u>most of the acts are symbolic</u>, a power struggle being described in apparently harmless acts and words.

Explore

Before reading on, think for yourself what the symbolic power is of Eddie's sparring with Rodolpho, Rodolpho's decision to resume dancing and Marco's challenge with the chair.

Almost nothing happens, yet this is a <u>fitting climax</u> to an act in which we have seen hints of desperate tragedy. There is an apparently light-hearted conversation, with Beatrice even reverting to the dizzy sit-com character of happier days ('I didn't know they're sardines!'). After some discussion of life in an Italian village, Eddie launches into an attack on Rodolpho's courtship of Catherine, but his language is now more moderate. Marco accepts his rulings and everything subsides. The young people dance to a record of *Paper Doll*. Eddie controls himself (though with difficulty, ripping his newspaper) just before his character assassination of Rodolpho goes too far and then the party settles down to some gentle horse-play: sparring, dancing and weight-lifting. That is what happens <u>on the surface</u>; what is symbolised is full of menace and meaning.

> **They went to Africa once. On a fishing boat.**

Eddie is restrained at first, but every word and gesture represents his <u>refusal to accept</u> Rodolpho in the happy family setting. When Catherine mentions that the men went to Africa, Eddie gives a significant glance and she defends herself: 'It's true, Eddie.' What is the meaning of that glance?

Text commentary

Certainly the meaning of his next few speeches is clear enough: every one is **pointedly addressed** to Marco and, the moment Rodolpho speaks, Eddie rounds on him. Marco talks about his wife and Eddie listens patiently until Rodolpho joins in, whereupon Eddie makes a **crude comment** about unfaithful wives and 'a couple extra' kids. To Eddie, **Rodolpho symbolises a woman-stealer**; his comment follows instinctively.

> **❝ It ain't so free here either, Rodolpho, like you think. ❞**

'It's more strict in our town,' says Rodolpho, explaining the absence of unexpected children. Eddie is thus given an excuse to explain that Rodolpho is behaving wrongly towards Catherine – if 'explain' is the right word for such a grinding out of prejudices. Note how he pretends to be discussing a general situation ('I seen greenhorns sometimes get in trouble that way'), but makes his meaning so clear that both Rodolpho and Beatrice respond by referring to Rodolpho. So far there is **no open hostility**: Eddie holds back his anger and constantly checks that Marco understands and agrees with him.

Most interesting is the response of Marco to Eddie's thinly disguised comments. Examine what he says on pages 53 and 54 ('No, Beatrice, if he does wrong you must tell him' to 'That's why we came') and consider what Marco's feelings are at this time and his **reasons** for speaking as he does.

> **❝ He senses he is exposing the issue and he is driven on. ❞**

As so often in Arthur Miller's plays, the **stage directions** are the key to much understanding. Essential to a great performance in a Miller play is the ability to reveal what is beneath the surface of the character.

Here we may ask ourselves whether Eddie wishes to behave so appallingly or whether he simply cannot avoid it. Read through the stage directions relating to Eddie from when he goes to his rocking chair (page 54) to asking Marco about boxing (page 56). Apart from his words (about Rodolpho's 'feminine' qualities), his looks and movements reveal a man in the grip of an obsession.

66 You wanna dance, Rodolpho? 99

From the point when Catherine puts on a record to dance to, almost every act is chosen by the character to bear an extra meaning. This is an important moment for Catherine who has always wished not to hurt Eddie. Much as she enjoys dancing with Rodolpho, that is not the reason for doing it or for choosing this record, *Paper Doll*. What do you think dancing to *Paper Doll* symbolises to Catherine? Again the clue is in the stage directions.

Explore

Though a much older song, *Paper Doll* was a huge hit for the Mills Brothers in the 1940s. They are probably the 'beautiful quartet' that Catherine refers to.

Eddie mounts his next attack verbally and the symbolism is obvious. He is pretending to say that singing, cooking and making dresses open up opportunities for Rodolpho; he means that they are signs of his effeminacy.

Look carefully at Eddie's behaviour in the boxing lesson. Firstly, it is a less unlikely way to behave than we might think; 'the fights' were a regular entertainment for working men and many escaped from the docks or the factories by their boxing talent. Eddie is more friendly to Rodolpho and speaks to him by name (a rarity for Eddie) and by nickname ('Danish', for his blond hair). He does not really hurt Rodolpho and avoids humiliating comments. All the points he is making are symbolic, not real. Consider what the symbolic implications of the sparring session are: they are far more than simply, 'I'm tougher than you are.'

Marco responds at last: family loyalty is greater than his concern not to irritate his benefactor, Eddie. In fact, the first symbolic response comes from Rodolpho. He denies that Eddie hurt him ('with a certain gleam and a smile') and then calmly moves to his own <u>act</u> of <u>defiance</u>. When Catherine asked him to dance before, he tried to refuse, 'in deference to Eddie'. Now he invites her to dance and the song is still *Paper Doll*.

Symbolically he is saying that the 'paper doll' is going to stand up for himself and that Eddie will achieve nothing by his bullying. As the 'paper doll' is a symbol of Rodolpho, so his dancing to the song shows that he is more than just a paper doll. If any doubt remains that Eddie has lost control of the situation, Marco's success with the chair reasserts family honour and represents strength, rejection of Eddie's bullying and, ultimately, <u>triumph</u>.

> **❝Eddie's grin vanishes as he absorbs his look.❞**

Explore

'I wanted to see whether I could write a play with one single arch instead of three acts ... I wanted to have one long line with one explosion, which is rather like the Greek way.' Arthur Miller

Not surprisingly, in a play where movement and gesture tell us so much, Act One ends not with a dramatic curtain line, but with a series of actions and reactions. Why did Arthur Miller choose to end Act One here? Initially, we know, he wrote the play without an interval, but it grew beyond the one-act version.

Whatever he originally planned, here (slightly beyond the half-way point) is where he chose to place the interval. What does he want the audience to think about? What do you anticipate in Act Two? Think back to the scene where the immigrants arrive and compare the behaviour of all five characters in that scene and in the final scene of the act. Has <u>the</u> <u>centre</u> <u>of</u> <u>the</u> <u>family</u> shifted?

Who? What? Why? When? Where? How?

1   Who go bowling together in Flatbush Avenue?

2   What did Rodolpho do with Catherine's old dress?

3   Why did Rodolpho refuse to dance with Catherine at first?

4   When did Eddie work in Hoboken, Staten Island, the West Side and Jersey?

5   Where did Alfieri go to try to get advice and help with Eddie's problems?

6   How does Brooklyn surprise Rodolpho?

Who said ... about whom?

1   '...he's a regular bull.'

2   'His eyes were like tunnels.'

3   'You think I'm jealous of you, honey?'

4   '...if he's here for a good time, then he could fool around!'

5   '...a son-of-a-bitch punk like that – which he came out of nowhere!'

6   'You're like a father to him!' (two people)

Open quotes

Find and complete the following:

1   'Well, he ain't exackly funny, but...'

2   'Girls don't have to wear black dress...'

3   'But if you act like a baby and he...'

4   'It's almost three months...'

What the characters don't know

Who: 1 has never seen Broadway?

2 suggests catching sardines on a hook?

3 has strange ideas about the colour of oranges?

Act Two

Pages 59–65

> **On the twenty-third of that December a case of Scotch whisky slipped from a net while being unloaded...**

Generally, dates and times are approximate in Act One. We are told the time, but not the date of the immigrants' arrival, and the argument after the visit to the Paramount takes place 'a couple of weeks' later, but there is little solid information. Act Two is different.

The chorus makes an **announcement**, setting the scene precisely for the important events that are imminent. The date is December 23rd; the whisky is Scotch; the pier it was being unloaded at is No. 41; the weather is cold, without snow. For these **momentous events**, we must have precise indications. The formal announcement is humanised at the end by Alfieri's reference to a later conversation with Catherine. The **precise dating** continues throughout Act Two: on December 27th, just after 6 o'clock, Eddie visits Alfieri and rings Immigration. The final tragedy takes place on the following Saturday. Unlike Act One, Act Two has the audience metaphorically reaching for a calendar as the action accelerates.

Explore

How much time has passed between Acts One and Two? Long enough for the syndicate to be paid off, we presume, otherwise Rodolpho would be working.

> **All the answers are in my eyes, Catherine.**

Rodolpho has changed; or is it just that we have never seen him alone with Catherine before? He speaks with **a new confidence and maturity**. The opening of the act tells us, with astonishing economy, how different he is from Eddie's perception, or even from Alfieri's references to him: '**the boy**'. As the lights rise, he is watching Catherine arrange a paper pattern (not dressmaking himself). Immediately and concisely, he expresses <u>his desire for Catherine</u>: he is hungry for her love, either immediately (as nearly happens shortly afterwards) or in a speedy marriage (as his next lines suggest). His reference to the money, 'I have nearly three hundred dollars', is payment for the marriage, certainly, but it also indicates that Rodolpho has been working for some time and has been <u>saving sensibly</u>. Compare this with Eddie's suspicions about what Rodolpho was doing with his money, and find some lines in Act One which Rodolpho has proved to be wrong.

Throughout Act One he has been the 'kid', the impetuously naïve one for whom allowances have to be made. In this scene he is the more mature one, coaxing Catherine to share his <u>maturity of attitude</u> <u>and</u> <u>emotion</u>.

> **❝** Would you still want to do it if it turned out we had to go live in Italy? **❞**

This is the <u>test question</u> that Eddie has told Catherine to ask Rodolpho: Can we live in Italy when we are married? An affirmative answer would show that he really loves her, that he is not just looking for citizenship. But would it? Would it show her that he really loved her if he took her to a country he himself has been unable to survive in?

Rodolpho gives a much better answer which is worth reading again in the speeches beginning 'There's nothing!', 'No, I will not marry you to live in Italy' and 'I am furious!'. In these you can see Rodolpho's <u>pride in himself and in his country</u> and his <u>loving responsibility</u> as a husband.

Explore

According to the rather preposterous *Dictionary of Races of People*, published in 1911 by the US Immigration Commission, Southern Italians were 'violent, undisciplined and incapable of genuine assimilation'.

To what extent does Rodolpho speak like an American? The question of language is intriguing in this play. Of course, the fact that most of the characters are uneducated and possibly were brought up speaking Italian means that there is <u>no need for a huge contrast</u> between the speech of the

Italians and that of the Americans. Marco is very silent in any case, and, on their first arrival, a few inversions ('Thousand-lire notes they threw from the tables') give a <u>slight</u> <u>sense</u> <u>of</u> <u>the</u> <u>foreign</u> in Rodolpho.

Now that he is at home in the country and with the language, Rodolpho's <u>imaginative</u> <u>personality</u> bursts out in <u>poetic</u> <u>language</u>: the gentle romance of 'If I take in my hands a little bird…'; the intense <u>metaphor</u> (an implied comparison) of 'I would be a criminal stealing your face'; the pride and passion of the repeated questions: 'Do you think I am so desperate?' He may not be an American yet, but how eloquent he is in the Americans' language!

> **"I'm not a baby, I know a lot more than people think I know. "**

Catherine seems <u>immature</u> <u>and</u> <u>inarticulate</u> compared with Rodolpho, but is that a <u>fair</u> <u>assessment</u>? Her talk of living in Italy is all rather foolish; she thinks Rodolpho could go to Rome and sing (on the strength of one night deputising for Andreola!) and that there *must* be jobs somewhere (despite everything Marco and Rodolpho have said). Are her motives so foolish? Maybe she just wants Rodolpho to say the word (that <u>she</u> <u>matters</u> <u>more</u> <u>than</u> <u>a</u> <u>passport</u>) so that they can stay in Brooklyn.

Explore

Explore the sort of language used by Catherine here (the broken sentences, the simple phrases, the girlish slang). It is quite different from the poetry of Rodolpho, but they get to the same place ('I love you, Rodolpho).

Catherine says, 'I'm afraid of Eddie here.' She is <u>shrewd</u> enough to see that Eddie could ruin their marriage, while at the same time being <u>generous</u> enough to admit what he has done for her. She is <u>cunning</u> enough to know that Eddie can be deceived ('Tell him you'd live in Italy – just tell him') and <u>loving</u> enough to want him to be happy. In the speeches from 'It's only that I…' to 'I don't know why I have to do that, I mean.' (page 62), Catherine expresses the <u>depth</u> <u>of</u> <u>her</u> <u>love</u> <u>for</u> <u>Eddie</u> at the moment that she knows she must give it up – and that is why she weeps.

Things are **never quite as straightforward** as they appear in the world of Arthur Miller's plays. Catherine, the innocent, suddenly reminds us with unexpected shrewdness that it is naïve to think of Eddie as a villain, Beatrice as a long-suffering saint, etc. Re-read the 'Then why don't she be a woman?' speech and penetrate beneath the childish vocabulary to an **interesting alternative view of the Carbone marriage**.

> **"** *Get your stuff and get outa here.* **"**

Rodolpho and Catherine move together in a mood of gentle inevitability. 'And don't cry any more' should be a farewell to emotional anguish and a promise of **security and fulfilment**. It is at this point that Eddie enters and everything changes.

Lights go up in the street in contrast to the withdrawal into the shadows of the bedroom. Eddie is **loud and staggering** in contrast to the gentleness that the lovers have reached. Above all, note how Miller deliberately overdoes the whisky: three bottles in different pockets. Eddie has taken his share of the cargo for Christmas, of course, but the impression is of a man who has been drinking enough for three.

Explore

In two others plays from Miller's great quartet of early plays, *All My Sons* and *Death of a Salesman*, different forms of paternal guilt lead to suicide. What happens to Eddie from here onwards could also be called self-destruction.

Considering that these are physical and passionate people, their **violent emotions have not yet led to violent action**: even the boxing match was more **symbolic** than a real contest. At the end of this short section, Eddie knows that he **cannot now avoid violent action** unless Catherine and Rodolpho give way.

'Don't make me do nuttin',' he pleads with Catherine, and he threatens Rodolpho, 'Just get outa here and don't lay another hand on her unless you wanna go out feet first.' However, everything the pair have said to him makes it clear that they do not accept his demands (for Catherine to stay and Rodolpho to go) and **his threats merely strengthen their resolve**.

We are now moving rapidly towards action: the symbolic acts are now more **explicit** and **violent** (the two kisses are accompanied by real, if brief, fighting) and not one line of dialogue is wasted.

Miller does not concern himself with wrong conclusions or feeble excuses; it is obvious what is going on (both enter from the bedroom, Catherine adjusting her dress), neither denies it and the scene begins with 'Get your stuff and get outa here'. What Miller is interested in is not the **evidence** for dismissing Rodolpho, but the **reaction** to that dismissal.

> **❝I think I have to get out of here, Eddie ❞**

Let us examine Catherine first. Immediately she says that she will have to leave as well; note that she _has_ to _leave_, not that she _wants to_. What does this show us about her feelings, both for Eddie and for Rodolpho? Then, in the speech beginning 'I think I can't stay here no more', she repeats the same ideas several times. Examine this speech (including the stage directions) and decide what Catherine feels for Eddie at this point.

Eddie responds instantly by **kissing** her. There are many reasons for this (the whisky he has drunk, for one thing), but it also has the symbolic force of saying, 'You ain't goin' nowheres' in action, not words.

Now Rodolpho must react, and this is equally sudden: the clear statement, 'She'll be my wife', followed by an attack on Eddie which he knows to be **hopeless**, but which is **unavoidable** after Eddie's taunting. Rodolpho must fight Eddie **to prove his manhood**. Why does Eddie choose to pin Rodolpho's arms and then **kiss him**, instead of seizing the opportunity to beat him up? Is it to prove a point to Catherine about Rodolpho? Instead it proves a point to Catherine about Eddie.

Explore

Eddie claims to Alfieri that Rodolpho's failure to break from the kiss reveals that he 'ain't right'. Strange logic from the kisser!

Where does this leave the main characters: Catherine horrified, Eddie torn between laughter and tears, Rodolpho rigid? Consider the stage directions: 'like animals that have torn at one another and broken off <u>without a decision</u>'. So the intended humiliation of Rodolpho has not come off: why not?

Explore

'One knew in the beginning more or less what was going to happen by the end and I liked that a lot because what was really involved was not *what* was going to happen, but *how* it was going to happen.'
Arthur Miller

The opening of Act Two provides both a major turning-point and <u>a scene of huge dramatic impact</u>. The four domestic scenes in Act One have wound up the tension, through words, symbolic gestures and body language (often detailed in the stage directions). Act Two is a much shorter act, with <u>increasing tempo</u> and <u>exploding tension</u> in two scenes of violent action: the arrest and Eddie's death. The first seven pages take us from the world of <u>slow tension</u> to the world of <u>explosive action</u>. By pages 64 and 65 discussion has been replaced by exclamation, question, broken sentences, outbursts of action and open confrontation.

Pages 65–67

The key moment in the play is dealt with very briefly and in a very low-key manner. The impact of the scene depends on all that has gone before, so that the telephone call becomes an <u>inevitable consequence</u>. It also depends on the actor playing Eddie. He is required to convey a <u>driven intensity</u> (from Alfieri's description) despite being given little to say and little to do.

> **❝I seem to tell this like a dream.❞**

The scene can be so brief partly because of Alfieri's manner of narrating. These events are <u>fated</u>: he now knows why he waited so long at the office. He is unable to break the grip of fate ('almost transfixed'/'I had lost my strength'). <u>The inevitability of tragedy</u> is expressed in the feeling that he wants to call the police, although nothing has happened. He can hardly remember the conversation, so he only gives us a bit of it. What he can remember is the impression that Eddie made: the dark room, the eyes like tunnels. Before this brief scene starts, the audience knows everything: <u>Alfieri's powerlessness</u>, <u>Eddie's destiny</u>, the unreality of the whole thing, even the way Eddie should look.

> **I'm warning you – the law is nature.**

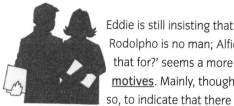

The scene is <u>cut off</u> at both ends. 'So in other words, he won't leave?' picks up an ongoing conversation. We are distracted from Alfieri's final words by the light rising on the telephone box – light for the next scene of the play, but also a <u>mysterious, menacing glow</u>. Alfieri questions perfunctorily, but we know (as he does) that the law has nothing to offer Eddie. Alfieri's most important speech actually spells out <u>natural moral law</u>: 'The law is only a word for what has a right to happen.'

Eddie is still insisting that the kissing episode shows that Rodolpho is no man; Alfieri's question, 'What did you do that for?' seems a more telling questioning of <u>hidden motives</u>. Mainly, though, this is a 'non-scene', deliberately so, to indicate that there is <u>no way out</u>.

> **Illegal immigrants. Two of them.**

Explore

'... in the middle of the McCarthy period ... the idea of a person who informs on his former associates and friends was in the air...' **Arthur Miller**

The telephone scene is again as brief as possible. With <u>a hint of a dream</u>, Eddie is lured towards the telephone as light rises on the booth and Alfieri's desperate, anguished calls fade into the darkness. The only extra added to the bare facts of the call is the appearance of <u>Louis and Mike, going about their normal business</u>: bowling again. Think about why Arthur Miller included them at this point.

> **I want my respect, Beatrice, and you know what I'm talkin' about.**

A constant theme in these pages is <u>Eddie's</u> <u>need</u> <u>for</u> <u>respect</u>, whether from his wife or from the community. You can no doubt think of reasons why, at this time, respect is even more important to him than formerly. At first it is prompted by Beatrice's lack of attention to his continued denial that Catherine is moving out. Any talk about respect between Eddie and Beatrice has as an underlying theme his failures as a husband, his <u>non-existent</u> <u>sex</u> <u>life</u>. Now he states, with massive arrogance (or is it just nervous defiance?) 'I do what I feel like doin' or what I don't feel like doin''. Though grammatically he is saying something else, the intended sense is clear enough.

Once he finds out about the other immigrants, Eddie's concern for his own reputation drives him to panic. Immediately he claims that Marco and Rodolpho might be caught in a sweep for the others ('How do you know they're not trackin' these guys?'). <u>Ironically,</u> <u>he</u> <u>betrays</u> <u>himself</u> in the attempt to clear himself.

In the end Eddie insists that <u>Marco</u> <u>should</u> <u>apologise</u> to him, protesting to the assembled neighbours that the accusations are false and being reduced to trying to get a nod or a word from Louis and Mike: 'He's gonna take that back.'

Explore

Eddie's concern with his good name can be compared to John Proctor in Miller's *The Crucible*: 'Because it is my name'. Proctor, though, is acting honourably.

It is too late: Eddie no longer has any reputation, respect or honour. In Act One, talking about <u>Vinny</u> <u>Bolzano</u>, Eddie told us what happens to a man who forfeits his honesty. Can you find words from that speech that summarise Eddie's loss of respect now?

> **They're going to get married next week**

Text commentary

Eddie will not attend the wedding. To begin with, he can't even talk to Catherine; he knows something the others don't, of course. As for Catherine, she is willing for Eddie to attend the wedding, but hardly enthusiastic.

How does Beatrice respond to this unpromising situation? Examine what she says about the wedding on pages 70 and 71. What does Beatrice want out of this whole sorry business? Is she seeking to lower Eddie's respect? Is there any truth in Eddie's claim on page 69 that she has changed ('It's a shootin' gallery in here and I'm the pigeon.')?

66 *Immigration! Open up in there!* 99

The main effect of the arrival of the immigration men needs no explanation. Activity and movement, questions and pursuits, fury and grief all create <u>a</u> <u>very</u> <u>dramatic</u> <u>scene</u>. In production it all happens very quickly, of course, but a good director will not allow the pace to blur the details.

<u>Dramatic</u> <u>irony</u> is when the audience knows something that the characters on stage do not. Here, for example, there is a <u>double entry</u> for the men from Immigration. They enter the composite set (looking for the right house?) while Eddie rages about moving Marco and Rodolpho and about his sacrifices for his family. We know they are there, but there is a <u>time-lapse</u> before they knock on the door and ruin Eddie's attempt at escape.

Are the men from Immigration presented as reasonable representatives of law and order, or as henchmen? There are <u>human</u> <u>touches</u>: they are called Dominick and Charley. Charley is local (he was born at 111, Union Street) and speaks a touch of Italian to them, though he translates *andiamo* for our benefit. Is their response to Catherine's protestations human or soulless? It is worth noting the <u>'last, informative look'</u> that the first officer gives Eddie after he has broken up the scuffle between him and Marco.

What's the matter with you, don't you believe I could think of your good? Did I ever ask sump'm for myself?

Eddie's reaction to the news of the Liparis' relations means that, when the Immigration officers arrive, he is in the middle of a flood of <u>passionate, but</u> <u>meaningless, self-justification</u>. Not surprisingly his main concern is to maintain his reputation. He can see a situation where, at best, an entire neighbourhood will ignore him. At worst, he will be involved in <u>two blood feuds</u> (one with Marco and Rodolpho, one with the Liparis), with nobody on his side. The reactions of the others share a general grief, but are not exactly the same.

Eddie's terror betrays his dark secret to Beatrice. Her <u>horrified disbelief</u> can express itself only by calling on God. Catherine bolts from the room when the officers arrive (why?) with a 'sob of fury'. Now compare the behaviour of Beatrice and Catherine when the officers bring down the immigrants. Which one is more aggressive? What is each trying to do? Compare the sentences that each of them repeats.

Marco's two rushes at Eddie, to spit at him and to point at him as a murderer, are the most striking happenings of the scene, but it is also worth looking at the words that Marco uses. In his disgust he is quite unable to name Eddie (he becomes 'that one') and even in his fury Marco remains the <u>family man</u> everyone admired so much in Act One: it is for his children that Marco curses Eddie.

Alfieri is <u>not the only choric figure</u>. The people of the neighbourhood also serve to reflect public opinion and tell us what to think. The Liparis make symbolic gestures: keening (wailing, as for the dead), kissing their relatives, turning from Eddie. Neither they nor Louis and Mike speak, but that is what is important. We must notice <u>the fact that they do not speak</u>.

Who? What? Why? When? Where? How?

1 *Who was working at dressmaking on December 23rd?*

2 *What was Beatrice packing in a box when Eddie came in?*

3 *Why did Alfieri stay late at the office?*

4 *When is the wedding of Catherine and Rodolpho to be?*

5 *Where precisely does Eddie live?*

6 *How does Catherine react to Eddie kissing Rodolpho?*

'You think we have no...?'

*When Rodolpho is 'furious', he tells Catherine that all Italy lacks is work. He lists **five** things that you can find in Italy. How many can you remember?*

Who said ... about whom?

1 *'I don't say you must hate him.' (two people)*

2 *'They got a temper, that family.'*

3 *'He was born in Philadelphia.'*

4 *'I gave them the blankets off my bed.'*

5 *'Cause in her heart she still loves you.' (two people)*

6 *'I would be a criminal stealing your face.'*

Open quotes

Find and complete the following:

1 *'He's gonna take that back or...'*

2 *'Even those who understand will...'*

3 *'I want you to be my wife, and...'*

4 *'Andiamo, andiamo...'*

This short scene is a contrast, in its stillness, with the explosive action before and after. It is simply a conversation, with minimal action, but it is nevertheless important. It shows the passage of time from the last scene and offers a brief rest from the passion and violence: to follow the arrest directly with the final scene would not work dramatically. It also reminds us, in a rather more calm way, of the essential themes of the play.

> *What will I tell him? He knows such a promise is dishonourable.*

As with Alfieri's scenes with Eddie, this scene begins in mid-conversation. In each case Alfieri is asking a question which is, in some way, a repeat of one previously asked. This question is all about Marco's sense of honour. Marco wishes to be bailed, but to be bailed he must give a promise not to harm Eddie. Which is more dishonourable: to break that promise or to allow Eddie to escape? 'You're an honourable man, I will believe your promise,' says Alfieri. Now read Alfieri's words and the stage directions associated with him at the end of this scene (pages 79–80) and decide if he is still so confident. Marco, on the other hand, dwells on honour of a different kind: this promise, he says, is 'dishonourable'. Eddie has degraded his blood (meaning his family) and robbed his children.

Marco sees it as his family duty to take revenge. He is not seeking financial compensation, but a restoration of family honour: like Eddie later, he deceives himself into thinking his enemy may wish to apologise. If so, this is enough: the name, the reputation, is restored.

Explore

Compare this with the Alfieri/Eddie scenes. See what comparisons you can make between Marco's and Eddie's questions and Alfieri's statements about the law, especially with Alfieri's opening speech of the play. Note the similarity between the scene endings on pages 67 and 79–80.

Text commentary

Opposed to this is the law. Marco cannot understand America: 'In my country he would be dead now', he says. Most tellingly he cannot understand that 'to promise not to kill is not dishonourable'. The **two concepts of justice** are offered in debate in simple, telling terms. Why is there no law against a man who has ruined a family? Is all the law in a book, as Alfieri says? Is justice something that can only come from God?

> ❝*When she marries him he can start to become an American.*❞

Marco cannot adjust from his old codes of honour. Rodolpho has already adjusted to 'settling for half' and, with Catherine, puts forward **practical reasons** for Marco to promise not to harm Eddie: they both want him at the wedding. The opportunity to work is also mentioned, giving Alfieri the chance to confirm that the hearing is a formality: Marco will be deported. He also confirms that, after the wedding, Rodolpho 'can start to become an American': he will stay. In the middle of a scene in which Marco's capacity for aggression is evident, note the **gentle satisfaction** with which he greets his brother's success. Before the final violent scene and Alfieri's brief epitaph for Eddie, the **remaining plot lines** are cleared up: we already know what will happen after the play finishes. What do you think is gained by this?

Pages 80–85

> ❝*Marco is coming, Eddie. He's praying in the church. You understand?*❞

The characters in the play are all **Roman Catholics** and, though references to it are fairly infrequent, we can sense that **religion is an important part** of their lives. There is, for instance, the frequent use of the word 'bless' (Catherine early on says that Rodolpho 'blesses' Eddie; Eddie pleads with Catherine, saying he only 'blesses' her). The word means more than just 'love' or 'approve of'; it is calling down God's blessing to make sure all goes well. In Alfieri's scene with Marco, there is again much emphasis on God as the only source of justice.

Here the religion is **more clear-cut**. The church is going to bless the wedding of Catherine and Rodolpho, but Marco is also asking for God's blessing on what to him is an honourable action. His prayer is like one before battle, or a bull-fighter in the chapel before entering the ring; it is a prayer for God's blessing **in success** **or** **in death**. Rodolpho, bringing the news of Marco praying, checks, 'You understand?' and they do.

66 *Then we all belong in the garbage.* 99

Text commentary

Eddie is guilty, that is obvious, but is **Eddie** *alone* **guilty**? Catherine, who held on to her love for him longer than seemed possible, now rounds on him in the lines beginning, 'Who the hell do you think you are?'

The violence of language is the **more shocking** coming from the mouth of Catherine. The **imagery** is powerful and dwells on animals, poison and disease. Eddie, she says, has no right to tell anyone anything, he is a poisonous sewer rat, he belongs with the other rubbish, he is outside the society of decent people. Beatrice's response is surprising. If Eddie belongs in the garbage, they all do, she says, because 'whatever happened we all done it.' Consider this statement. Is it true? *Are* they all to blame? Is Beatrice merely trying to calm Eddie down? Is her view distorted by her love for him? Whatever you decide, this is not a statement to be dismissed lightly.

Explore

A regular theme for Arthur Miller is taking responsibility for your actions. For example, Chris in *All my Sons* says: 'there's a universe of people outside and you're responsible to it...'.

66 *It is my fault, Eddie.* 99

Rodolpho's behaviour at this point is remarkable. He wishes to apologise <u>for</u> <u>failing</u> <u>to</u> <u>ask</u> <u>permission</u> for Catherine and for bringing all the troubles, but he is <u>not</u> <u>without</u> <u>pride</u>. He states that Eddie insulted him, too, but he does not require an apology. He is <u>willing to</u> <u>forgive</u>: 'Maybe God understand why you did that to me.' All that matters now is comradeship, symbolised by the kissing of the hand, which Eddie does not accept.

Explore

You can compare the kiss that Eddie refuses (a kiss of the hand in reconciliation) with the kiss that he took violently (a kiss on the lips to express contempt and rejection).

Rodolpho's conduct is the opposite of the code of honour which is currently driving Marco and Eddie, <u>an</u> <u>explicit</u> <u>rejection</u> <u>of</u> <u>the</u> <u>blood</u> <u>feud</u>. Which do you find the more honourable? Is there a place for forgiveness?

> **66** *Animal! You go on your knees to me!* **99**

Marco kills Eddie after refusing to follow the reasonable arguments of Alfieri, Catherine and Rodolpho. He has gone back on his word to Alfieri. Does that make him a <u>villain</u>? It is certainly hard to accept Marco as a villain: even Eddie, we are reminded, 'always liked Marco'. Miller does not tell us that Marco is found guilty of murder; quite possibly, he is merely deported, as would have happened anyway. But look at the methods Miller uses to <u>blur</u> <u>Marco's</u> <u>guilt</u>. Almost his last words to Alfieri are 'Maybe he wants to apologise to me', so perhaps that is why he is coming to see Eddie. So why go to church first? Maybe he fears Eddie will provoke a fatal struggle. Not very convincing, but <u>enough</u> <u>to</u> <u>blur</u> <u>our</u> <u>certainty</u> … and what do you think would have been Marco's reaction to an apology?

When he arrives, he speaks only once (to call 'Eddie Carbone!' – the name, symbol of respect and honour) and no indication is given of his aggressive mood or actions until Eddie moves for him. Then, calling Eddie an animal, he strikes him down: again, the symbolism is all-important – Eddie on his knees to Marco. The lethal knife, of course, comes from Eddie. Just how guilty is Marco? You would be naïve to think that he was coming to have a pre-wedding chat with Eddie, but there are levels of guilt and layers of honour.

"The truth is not as bad as blood, Eddie!"

There is a <u>double</u> <u>climax</u> to the play: <u>truth</u> <u>and</u> <u>blood</u>. On page 83 the two follow in immediate sequence. Beatrice finally says, 'You want somethin' else, Eddie, and you can never have her!' Catherine is horrified, Eddie is described as shocked, horrified, agonised, crying out, clenching his bursting head, refusing to believe that Beatrice would think that of him. And then Marco calls his name.

So we need to find our way through the double climax of truth and blood by examining <u>Eddie's</u> <u>words</u> <u>and</u> <u>actions</u>. To begin with, he is doggedly convinced that he is in the right: Marco must apologise to him. If Beatrice goes to the wedding, she need not come back; they are either on his side or against him. He responds to Catherine's insults by nearly throwing the table at her: what does that suggest about his state of mind? Eddie will not respond to the news of Marco or to Rodolpho's apology.

The reason Eddie gives is that he <u>wants</u> <u>his</u> <u>name</u>. Rodolpho is only a kid, a punk. What he does is of no account; only Marco can give him his name back and, if he doesn't, 'we have it out'. But now we have to question his motives: Beatrice says that Marco has nothing to give him. What he really wants is Catherine.

Explore

You may have studied *Macbeth*. If you have, think of Macbeth, weighed down by sins and deserted by his followers, going recklessly to his death. Is there any similarity between this and how Eddie is feeling?

Ask yourself now:
- Is the person Eddie needs to get his 'name' from really himself?
- Does he refuse to accept any peace-making because his real lack of peace is within himself?
- Does he now realise that he is doomed and resolve on a desperate last act?

In his speech, 'Maybe he comes to apologise to me...' Eddie gradually makes himself angry ('incensing himself') as he argues his version of events to the people of Red Hook. If they do not accept that he is right, he cannot live among them, so <u>Marco is accused three times of lying</u> and told (also three times) to admit it, or to give Eddie his name (the same thing). Every stage of the fight is <u>provoked by Eddie</u>, and his death comes swiftly. Both women support his body and call his name, but notice whose name *Eddie* calls, who protects his dead body in her arms. As Eddie dies, reflect on what <u>that final act of love</u> tells us about the tragedy. Reflect also on the significance (for the drama, for the character) of Catherine's last line.

❝ *I mourn him … with a certain … alarm* ❞

Text commentary

In <u>Alfieri's epitaph</u> we are taken back to the beginning: compare the words of Alfieri now and then. Eddie is finally the subject of the tragedy – not that he is the most heroic or sympathetic figure in the play, but he is the one with whose character and dilemma the audience has most fully identified, <u>the one whose force has driven the tragedy</u>. Alfieri's words are <u>the equivalent of a funeral sermon</u>, but they leave <u>questions, not certainties</u>. Why, in particular, does Alfieri feel as he does? He trembles and mourns Eddie with a certain alarm. He loves him more than his other clients, but finds this wrong and thinks that he should have settled for half. Why does Alfieri have these <u>contradictions</u>? Do you share them?

Explore

When the play was first produced, Miller was approached by many people who identified so fully that they were certain that they knew the original Eddie Carbone!

Who? What? Why? When? Where? How?

1   *Who tried to break up the fight until threatened with a knife?*

2   *What did Rodolpho do to symbolise his apology to Eddie?*

3   *Why did Alfieri require a promise from Marco?*

4   *When will Marco's tribunal be?*

5   *Where did Marco go before he went to Eddie's house?*

6   *How much chance does Marco have of remaining in America?*

Who said ... about whom?

1   *'If he obeys the law, he lives.'*

2   *'And so I mourn him – I admit it – with a certain... alarm.'*

3   *'It was wrong that I did not ask your permission.'*

4   *'He can't bail you out if you're gonna do something bad.' (two people)*

5   *'He bites people when they sleep.'*

6   *'Which he said I killed his children!'*

Open quotes

Find and complete the following:

1   *'Give me the satisfaction...'*

2   *'To come out of the water and...'*

3   *'...not purely good but...'*

4   *'Now gimme my name and...'*

5   *'Maybe God understand...'*

6   *'Eddie, I never meant to...'*

Writing essays for exams and coursework

- Time for examination essays is very limited: possibly 45 minutes, depending on the specification you are following.

- Preparation therefore needs to be thorough, so that you can remember information quickly.

- Simply telling the story is of very little use. Your essay will test your ability in at least one of the areas listed under **Coursework**.

- Your opening sentence/paragraph should state clearly the point you are making or the topic you are going to discuss, not relate an event.

- You will probably be allowed to take the text into the examination, but from 2004 you will definitely not be allowed to make notes in it.

- Looking up facts or quotations in the book wastes far too much time. Your revision must be thorough enough for you to find anything you need at once; you might, for instance, need to check the exact words of a quotation.

- Keep quotations short. If you learn those on pages 64–65, you should normally quote only a part of them.

- Paragraphing is very important. The opening sentence of each paragraph should state what it is about. Making sure that each paragraph is about something specific keeps you on the subject.

- Try very hard to avoid irrelevant information: there isn't time.

- In many ways the guidance is the same for coursework as for examinations: relevance, clear paragraphing, avoiding too much story-telling, etc. The difference is that you have more time in which to do it.

- You will be asked to show understanding, insight and the ability to analyse the text.

- You will need to write on one or more of: the effects of character and action; the effects of dramatic devices and structures (how it works as a play); layers of meaning in language, ideas and themes (getting beneath the surface); social, historical and cultural setting.

- Essays will be more substantial than in an examination, but don't make the mistake of thinking that the only way to an A* is to write an essay of enormous length: quality matters far more than quantity.

- You should aim for perfection in terms of organisation, relevance and accuracy. For this reason drafting is all-important.

- When re-drafting, be prepared to make substantial changes to the structure of the essay. Re-drafting is not just a matter of reading through and altering a few words.

- It is possible that your teacher will ask you to do an oral presentation (on your own or with a group) instead of an essay. If your oral task is part of your Literature coursework, you must make sure that you show the skills of analysis required for essays: you don't get good grades in Literature just by talking fluently and interestingly.

Writing essays

> *I don't understand you; she's seventeen years old, you gonna keep her in the house all her life?*

You need to know some quotation that reveals Eddie's unhealthy obsession with Catherine *even before Rodolpho comes on the scene*. This sentence from Beatrice (page 20) does that.

> *Right on the deck, all of a sudden, a whole song comes out of his mouth – with motions. You know what they're callin' him now? Paper Doll they're callin' him, Canary. He's like a weird.*

These words of Eddie (pages 34–35) are from one of many speeches that reveal his contempt for Rodolpho – and the lack of hard evidence for his assumptions.

> *You know, sometimes God mixes up the people. We all love somebody, the wife, the kids – every man's got somebody that he loves, heh? But sometimes there's too much. You know? There's too much, and it goes where it mustn't.*

This is Alfieri's classic statement of Eddie's problem (page 48). There are other parts of the same speech that are equally telling ('…too much love for the niece.').

> *But if I could cook, if I could sing, if I could make dresses, I wouldn't be on the water-front.*

Eddie (page 55) is building towards the Act One climax. When it comes, the climax is expressed more in action than in words, so you will need to refer to events like Marco lifting the chair rather than actual quotations.

> *How can I bring you from a rich country to suffer in a poor country? ... I would be a criminal stealing your face.*

Rodolpho explains to Catherine (page 60) why his desire to become an American citizen by marrying her is not just selfish opportunism, but sensible and loving.

> *You don't know him; he was always the sweetest guy to me. Good. He razzes me all the time but he don't mean it. I know. I would – just feel ashamed if I made him sad.*

A key element in Miller's subtle characterisation is Catherine's devotion (almost throughout) to Eddie, summed up here on page 62.

> *The law is only a word for what has a right to happen.*

One of Alfieri's many unsuccessful attempts (this one on page 66) to persuade Eddie (and, later, Marco) to accept the law as it exists.

> *I want my name! He didn't take my name; he's only a punk. Marco's got my name – and you can run tell him, kid, that he's gonna give it back to me in front of this neighbourhood, or we have it out.*

This is one of the statements by Eddie (page 82) that define what he and Marco are quarrelling about.

Most of you are likely to write about *A View from the Bridge* as coursework, rather than part of an examination, but it is possible that the play will be set as an examination text. If so, we can be sure that the questions will be of three types (though not every paper may contain all three):

● a response to an extended extract from the play;

● a question asking you to comment, criticise and analyse the play;

● a more imaginative piece asking you to re-create the play in some way.

For example:

1 *(Quotation: Alfieri's opening speech) How does Arthur Miller succeed, in this opening section, in capturing the audience's attention and setting out the main issues of the play?*

2 *What is the dramatic impact of the final scene of Act One? Consider the effect of the bout of sparring, Rodolpho dancing with Catherine and Marco's challenge to Eddie.*

3 *Imagine yourself to be Alfieri and write an account of your thoughts and concerns after the Act Two meeting with Eddie.*

4 *How important is the social background in Red Hook in understanding the way Eddie behaves?*

5 *How convincing is Miller's presentation of the relationship between Catherine and Rodolpho? You should consider the growing maturity of both characters as well as their feelings for each other.*

6 *Which character do you think changes and develops most in the course of the play? You will need to compare his or her character and behaviour early in the play and at the end and also consider how Arthur Miller uses language and dramatic devices to reveal the change.*

7 *(Quote the Immigration Officers scene pages 73 to 77)*

Analyse the dramatic effectiveness of this scene. You should consider the way Miller has built the tension towards this scene and how far it can be considered the climax to the play, as well as exploring the action in the scene itself. You need to comment on the significance of the words and actions of the various characters, including minor parts like the Liparis, Louis and Mike.

8 *Imagine yourself to be Catherine and write a letter to Alfieri, asking for his assistance in persuading Marco to be reasonable and agree to give up thoughts of revenge. Make sure that you reveal Catherine's feelings and opinions about other characters, notably Eddie, Beatrice and Rodolpho.*

9 *Analyse the relationships between Eddie, Beatrice and Catherine and consider how far the arrival of Marco and Rodolpho causes the tragedy. Would there have been a tragedy without them? Consider the dramatic impact of scenes involving Eddie, Beatrice and Catherine and examine the pressures placed on them by society.*

10 *Are Marco and Rodolpho convincing as a pair of brothers? Examine their relationship with each other, their reactions to life with Eddie and his family, and also the society that they belong to.*

In the case of any of these titles, you are likely to be helped by a series of bullet points listing matters which you may wish to consider.

These notes apply mainly to coursework essays. In an examination the process must obviously be quicker and briefer, though many of the same principles apply.

- First, be clear in your mind that you are not just 'writing about' *A View from the Bridge*. You are answering a specific question.

- Therefore, place the question in the centre of your thinking, just as it is in the centre of the mind maps on the next three pages.

- Start by thinking of all the helpful responses to the title that you can. Write them down without worrying about the order or how they fit together.

- Try to decide whether any of these responses are responding to other ideas rather than directly to the question, or which ones can be linked together. Mark on your plan which responses belong to the same 'family'.

- You can build up your plan in the form of a mind map similar to those that follow. The advantage of using a mind map is that it lets you expand your ideas in a clearly linked, very visual way.

- Now that you have plenty of ideas and some sense of form, decide which order would be best for your essay.

- You need an introduction, but it should take the reader into the answer, not just tell him/her about the play in general.

- Your arguments should lead on from each other, with similar ideas grouped together. Sometimes you may develop one point of view, then answer it or disagree.

- A conclusion as such may not be necessary, but make sure that the reader knows what your final opinion is.

- As stated on page 63, work through several drafts and be prepared to make substantial changes to material and structure. Only with the final draft is your main concern checking spelling, grammar, etc.

How does Arthur Miller convince the audience of the inevitability of the tragedy in *A View from the Bridge*?

Honour code
- Unwilling to accept law (Alfieri with Eddie/Marco)
  - No compromise
    - Unwilling to 'settle for half'

Family honour (involvement of Liparis)

Social background

Chorus
- Alfieri's linking commentary ('I could see every step...')
- Alfieri's opening speech ('run its bloody course')

Eddie's passion

History of violence
- Story of Vinny Bolzano
- Alfieri's account of gangsters

'I think I will love him more than all my sensible clients.' Is there any justification for regarding Eddie as a lovable character?

Eddie as much victim as villain

B's reaction to him
- But see her reaction to his death
- Marriage not working

Reveals himself as he really is – 'himself purely'

BUT

Prove ways in which he was wrong…

Catherine's reaction to him – 'always the sweetest guy to me'

Signs of the opposite?

Any signs during the play?

Is Alfieri saying he is 'lovable'?

Remainder of Alfieri's final speech: 'I know how wrong he was' 'not purely good'

Devoted family man Accounts of hard work certainly true

Compare and contrast the characters of the two brothers, Marco and Rodolpho. How do the differences between them add to the dramatic effect of the play?

Only obvious similarity – devoted to each other: 'Marco shakes him affectionately'/chair incident/ Rodopho looks to Marco for permission

Rodolpho's process of maturing alters the relationship

Key scene with Alfieri – Rodolpho mature and saying little

Marco being married accounts for some

How much of the difference is based on age?

Comparison is made constantly

Difference helps to suggest something strange about Rodolpho

Difficult in every obvious way

Talkative, fanciful, blond, making new life in America, regarded as 'weird'

Silent, matter-of-fact, dark, devoted to family in Italy, accepted in Red Hook

Marco originally buffer between Eddie and Rodolpho, giving tension time to develop

Irony of Marco as Eddie's killer

Eddie sees Marco as the 'right' brother

Sample response

How does Miller create dramatic tension in *A View from the Bridge*? You may range across the whole play or restrict yourself to an analysis of two or three key scenes.

In "A View from the Bridge" Miller creates dramatic tension by describing the settings✔ ; for example, 'The lights go down, then come up on Alfieri, who has moved onto the forestage.' I think that by doing this the writer has got the audience wondering✔ what is going to happen next and, because the lights are just on this one person, the audience has to focus✔ on what he is saying. It is important for the dramatic tension✔ to listen carefully to all Alfieri's speeches. He warns the audience about the fact that the Sicilians pay no attention to the law✔ and he tells us right at the beginning that Eddie is dangerous✔ and that he is 'powerless'✔ to stop the 'bloody course' of what will happen.

Miller creates dramatic tension by the way he changes from scene to scene✔ . Between every scene there is an interlude✔ that involves Alfieri, or sometimes Alfieri and another person. This creates a tense atmosphere between the audience and the actor who plays Alfieri. Alfieri knows what is going to happen✔ and his speech leaves the audience anticipating✔ what is going to happen, but uncertain✔ of how it will work out.

Miller also creates dramatic tension in the parts of the play where there is confrontation✔ , whether mental, physical or even both✔ . Often the tension has to come from the actors by means of the stage directions✔ . For example, in Act One, when Eddie lashes out at Catherine because of her relationship with Rodolpho, Beatrice 'looks past the sobbing Catherine at Eddie who, in the presence of his wife, makes an awkward gesture of eroded command, indicating Catherine.'

All three characters are highly emotional✔ and Beatrice is described as 'inwardly angered' at Eddie's emotion. This suggests to me that she feels that something is going on✔ between Eddie and Catherine. This builds up the sense of dramatic tension in the audience because Beatrice can't hide✔ what she's feeling about this. The tension is communicated to Eddie because he walks away 'in guilt'✔ .

In many scenes, actions✔ help to build up the tension. At the end of Act One, what Marco, Rodolpho, Catherine and Eddie do has a wider meaning✔ and shows that there is conflict✔ between them. Eddie pretends that he is only teaching Rodolpho to box✔ , but he hits him hard enough to warn him to stay away from Catherine. Rodolpho doesn't obey the warning and, when he starts dancing again, his defiance✔ of Eddie shows that there is conflict to come.

Dramatic tension exists between the characters✔ . This is especially true of Eddie because you can see signs of conflict✔ between him and all the other main characters, even when the scene is about something trivial✔ , like what time Catherine and Rodolpho come back from the cinema. Ironically, the only main character he has no quarrel with at first is Marco,✔ who finally kills him.

Besides the main characters dramatic tension comes from the setting and the lighting. Whenever the lights go down, you know that the scene is going to change or a new character is going to begin talking. Also, Alfieri and the minor characters ✓ like Mike, Louis and the Liparis remind us of what life is like in Red Hook ✓ and make us expect violence ✓.

Examiner's comments

This essay clearly shows understanding of the play and the issues, which means that it is worth at least a Grade D. There is just enough insight to justify a Grade C, with some good comment particularly on action and stage directions. The comments on the actual text are less successful. A good Grade C, or even a Grade B, needs much more awareness of how dramatic tension grows from character revelations in words spoken – backed up by better use of quotations. The essay stays reasonably on the subject and is fairly well paragraphed, but has no overall shape. It tends to be imprecise; for instance, the first quotation of a stage direction about Alfieri is not identified and, in fact, comes from a different scene from the one the candidate then writes about. The reference to the 'interludes' with Alfieri or 'Alfieri and another person' doesn't make clear the difference between Alfieri's choric commentary and the scenes where he appears as a character.

Sample response

How does Miller create dramatic tension in *A View from the Bridge*? You may range across the whole play or restrict yourself to an analysis of two or three key scenes.

"A View from the Bridge" centres predominantly around a poor Sicilian patriarchal community✓ . Their culture entails loyalty and family honour✓ at any cost. Miller has used these fierce cultural beliefs✓ as an aid to creating dramatic tension through the characters who are supposed to abide✓ by this notion. Miller cleverly shapes the audience's response by using dramatic irony✓ and tension throughout the play. He also uses characters with strong personalities✓ and potentially dangerous character flaws✓ to create dramatic tension.

The play's main focus is conflict✓ , with the first one being between Catherine and Eddie✓ . The conflict is a mental one about something physical. It is clear that Eddie is fond✓ of Catherine: he compliments her on her hairstyle, remarking 'beautiful'✓ . Eddie's more protective✓ nature is revealed when he comments on her short skirt and her high heels, saying, 'You are walkin' wavy!✓ I don't like the looks they're givin' you in the candy store.' Catherine tries to defend herself, but is reduced to tears.✓

This conflict portrays Eddie as possessive✓ and protective✓ over Catherine, which causes dramatic tension. The Sicilian male-dominated✓ society may be a reason why Eddie is so protective over his 18-year-old niece✓ . When Beatrice tells Eddie that Catherine has been offered a job, he is instantly cynical✓ and nervous✓ as well as angry. He stubbornly says he 'doesn't like the neighbourhood' and 'she'll be with a lotta plumbers.' This underlines his possessiveness✓ . Eventually Eddie gives in and becomes more relaxed. However, the audience is aware that his possessive nature has merely been temporarily drowned✓ and will inevitably resurface✓ . By exposing Eddie's character flaws✓ Miller is creating dramatic tension. The audience is aware that Eddie tries to shy away from the truth✓ about his feelings for Catherine and therefore an inevitable conflict✓ will eventually arise.

Miller also uses Alfieri as an aid to creating tension✓ throughout the play. He narrates and comments at key points✓ and he is also an active character✔ . His powerless status✔ makes the outcome of the story seem inevitable. Alfieri is portrayed as a powerless observer, which creates a sense of inevitable fate✔ and therefore tension.

Alfieri's primary role is as a commentator✔ , as when he introduces the play in the opening scene. Miller instantly begins to associate him with trouble✔ when Alfieri explains, 'We're only thought of in connection with disasters'. He is also a key part of describing the background✔ and setting of the play. The lawyer gives the impression that family honour✔ and respect are important within the Sicilian community✔ and that there is a great distrust of the law✔ . Miller has underlined the significance of honour and justice by saying, 'Justice is very important here✔ '. As an audience member you realise that this is potentially a key aspect✔ of the play. It subtly creates apprehension✔ about what will inevitably happen.

Finally, Alfieri concludes his introduction by saying, 'and sat there as powerless as I, and watched it run its bloody course', which makes the audience expect a tragic outcome✔ to be resolved in blood.✔ Throughout Alfieri's introduction there is a sense of dramatic tension and an inevitable destiny✔ . Miller slowly engages the audience with Alfieri's dramatic introduction and makes them feel apprehensive.

The society in which the characters live could potentially cause instability✔ and tension✔ . It is clear that it is a patriarchal✔ society, as Beatrice and Catherine serve Eddie and appear to be dominated✔ by him. This sort of male-dominated society in which women are suppressed and dependent on men could potentially create dramatic tension.

At the very end of Act One Eddie 'playfully' teaches Rodolpho to box. I think he does this to maintain his dominance✔ in the household and also to belittle✔ Rodolpho. Eddie almost patronises✔ him in an attempt to show that 'the guy ain't right'✔ . By this point in the play it is clear that there is a lot of friction✔ between Eddie and Rodolpho and that Eddie is jealous✔ of his relationship with Catherine. When Eddie punches Rodolpho, tension between Marco and Eddie emerges✔ . Marco asserts his power✔ by lifting a chair above his head which Eddie can barely lift off the ground. This is Marco's way of warning✓ Eddie not to mess with his family.

Again the idea of family loyalty✓ and honour✓ comes into play. Miller uses powerful symbolism✓ as Marco raises the chair and comes face to face with Eddie; the chair is 'raised like a weapon'✓. It is clear by the way 'Eddie's grin vanishes as he absorbs his look' that he feels threatened✓ by Marco and that it is only a matter of time✓ before an inevitable outcome✓ to the family's tension and conflict arises.

By looking at these few key scenes Miller's clever methods of creating dramatic tension are exposed. He uses the patriarchal Sicilian society's culture of family honour and loyalty at any cost as an aid to creating inevitability and tension✓. He also uses strong characters like Eddie and Marco as well as their personality flaws.

Examiner's comments

For Grade A analytical and interpretative skills are required and this piece clearly displays these. The candidate responds well to character and action, showing sensitivity to character, and has some success in analysing language. Particularly impressive is the consideration of social, cultural and historical background which becomes part of the main argument of the essay. The number of references to 'dramatic tension' may be a little monotonous, but it keeps the essay on subject throughout, and the use of quotations (brief, usually absorbed into the sentence) is very effective. There is little sign of the originality required for A* and the essay would have benefited from detailed examination of how words and actions create tension in individual scenes; most of the best analysis is of the inevitability of tragedy.

Answers to quick quizzes

Quick quiz 1

Who? What? Why? When? Where? How?

1   Vinny Bolzano (page 23)
2   sang at the hotel (page 31)
3   because they are on their own/because of the danger of immigration officers (page 26)
4   in four, five or six years (page 29)
5   in Nostrand Avenue by the Navy Yard (page 18)
6   because they owe the organisation money (page 27)

Who said ... about whom?

1   Marco about Rodolpho (page 31)
2   Marco about Tony, the man who brought them to Eddie's (page 27)
3   Alfieri about Al Capone (page 12)
4   Eddie about the Immigration Bureau (page 23)
5   Eddie about Catherine (page 20)
6   Rodolpho about Marco (page 29)

Open quotes

1   'And now we are quite civilised, quite American.' (page 12)
2   'The horses in our town are skinnier than goats.' (page 28)
3   '...she's seventeen years old, you gonna keep her in the house all her life?' (page 20)
4   'My wife – she feeds them from her own mouth.' (page 29)

What is...

1   the Underground or Metro
2   a large American car
3   a Mafia-type organisation

Quick quiz 2

Who said ... about whom?

1   Mike about Marco (page 37)
2   Alfieri about Eddie (page 45)
3   Beatrice about Catherine (page 44)
4   Eddie about Rodolpho (page 54)
5   Eddie about Rodolpho (page 49)
6   Catherine about Eddie and Rodolpho (page 40)

Who? What? Why? When? Where? How?

1   Mike and Louis (page 38)
2   Made a new one (page 47)
3   'in deference to Eddie' (page 54)
4   when there was no work ('empty piers') in Brooklyn (page 49)
5   a 'wise old woman' (page 50)
6   there are no fountains (page 39)

Open quotes

1   'Well, he ain't exackly funny, but he's always like making remarks like, y'know?' (page 37)
2   'Girls don't have to wear black dress to be strict.' (page 52)
3   'But if you act like a baby and he be treatin' you like a baby' (page 43)
4   'It's almost three months you don't feel good...' (page 36)

What the characters don't know

1   Rodolpho (page 39)
2   Beatrice (page 51)
3   Eddie (page 51)

Quick quiz 3

Who? What? Why? When? Where? How?

1. *Catherine (page 59)*
2. *Christmas decorations (page 67)*
3. *because he 'knew' Eddie would come, as he was fated to (page 65)*
4. *next week (page 70) or on Saturday (page 71)*
5. *441, Saxon Street, Brooklyn (page 67)*
6. *by attacking Eddie, tearing at his face/by threatening to kill him (page 64)*

'You think we have no…?'
tall buildings, electric lights, wide streets, flags, automobiles

Who said … about whom?

1. *Rodolpho about Catherine and Eddie (page 63)*
2. *Eddie about the Liparis (page 73)*
3. *Catherine about Rodolpho (page 75)*
4. *Eddie about Marco and Rodolpho (page 77)*
5. *Beatrice about Catherine and Eddie (page 70)*
6. *Rodolpho about Catherine (page 60)*

Open quotes

1. *'He's gonna take that back or I'll kill him.' (page 77)*
2. *'Even those who understand will turn against you.' (page 67)*
3. *'I want you to be my wife, and I want to be a citizen.' (page 61)*
4. *'Andiamo, andiamo, let's go.' (page 75)*

Quick quiz 4

Who? What? Why? When? Where? How?

1. *Louis (page 84)*
2. *tried to kiss his hand (page 82)*
3. *to obtain bail (page 78)*
4. *in five or six weeks (page 79)*
5. *to church (page 81)*
6. *none: the hearing is a formality (page 78)*

Who said … about whom?

1. *Alfieri about Eddie (page 79)*
2. *Alfieri about Eddie again (page 85)*
3. *Rodolpho about Eddie (page 82)*
4. *Catherine about Alfieri and Marco (page 78)*
5. *Catherine about Eddie (page 81)*
6. *Eddie about Marco (page 82)*

Open quotes

1. *'Give me the satisfaction – I want you at the wedding.' (page 78)*
2. *'To come out of the water and grab a girl for a passport?' (page 83)*
3. *'…not purely good, but himself purely.' (page 85)*
4. *'Now gimme my name and we go together to the wedding.' (page 84)*
5. *'Maybe God understand why you did that to me.' (page 82)*
6. *'Eddie, I never meant to do nothing bad to you.' (page 84)*

First published 1997
Revised edition 2004,
reprinted 2004, 2005
10 9 8 7 6 5 4 3

Letts Educational
The Chiswick Centre
414 Chiswick High Road
London W4 5TF
Tel: 0845 602 1937
Fax: 020 8996 8767

Text © Ron Simpson 1997 and 2004

Cover and text design by Hardlines Ltd, Charlbury, Oxfordshire.

Typeset by Letterpart Ltd, Reigate, Surrey.

Graphic illustration by Beehive Illustration, Cirencester, Gloucestershire.

Commissioned by Cassandra Birmingham

Editorial project management by Jo Kemp

Printed in Italy.

British Library Cataloguing in Publication Data. A CIP record of this book is
available from the British Library.

ISBN 1 84315 321 1

Letts Educational is a division of Granada Learning Limited,
part of Granada plc.